MW00911199

Cliff

Making Microsoft® Windows® Me Millennium Edition Work for You

By Brian Underdahl

IN THIS BOOK

- Getting started with Windows Me
- Connecting to the Internet
- Organizing your projects
- Customizing your computer
- Reinforce what you learn with CliffsNotes Review
- Find more information about Windows Me in the CliffsNotes Resource Center and online at www.cliffsnotes.com

IDG Books Worldwide, Inc.
An International Data Group Company
Foster City, CA • Chicago, IL • Indianapolis, IN • New York, NY

About the Author

Brian Underdahl has written or contributed to more than 48 books about computing. Brian also writes for magazines about computers, teaches numerous computer classes, and speaks to professional organizations.

Publisher's Acknowledgments

Editorial

Project Editor: Paul Levesque
Acquisitions Editor: David Mayhew
Copy Editor: Gwenette Gaddis
Proof Editor: Teresa Artman
Technical Editor: Allen Wyatt

Production

Proofreader: York Production Services, Inc.
Indexer: York Production Services, Inc.
IDG Books Indianapolis Production Department

CliffsNotes™ Making Microsoft® Windows® Me Millennium Edition Work for You

Published by

IDG Books Worldwide, Inc.

An International Data Group Company
919 E. Hillsdale Blvd.
Suite 400
Foster City, CA 94404
www.idgbooks.com (IDG Books Worldwide Web site)
www.cliffsnotes.com (CliffsNotes Web site)

Library of Congress Control Number: 00-103361

ISBN: 0-7645-8645-9

Printed in the United States of America

10 9 8 7 6 5 4 3 2 1

1V/SR/QX/QQ/IN

Distributed in the United States by IDG Books Worldwide, Inc.

Distributed by CDG Books Canada Inc. for Canada; by Transworld Publishers Limited in the United Kingdom; by IDG Norge Books for Norway; by IDG Sweden Books for Sweden; by IDG Books Australia Publishing Corporation Pty. Ltd. for Australia and New Zealand; by TransQuest Publishers Pte Ltd. for Singapore, Malaysia, Thailand, Indonesia, and Hong Kong; by Gotop Information Inc. for Taiwan; by ICG Muse, Inc. for Japan; by Intersoft for South Africa; by Eyrolles for France; by International Thomson Publishing for Germany, Austria and Switzerland; by Distribuidora Cuspide for Argentina; by LR International for Brazil; by Galileo Libros for Chile; by Ediciones ZETA S.C.R. Ltda. for Peru; by WS Computer Publishing Corporation, Inc., for the Philippines; by Contemporanea de Ediciones for Venezuela; by Express Computer Distributors for the Caribbean and West Indies; by Micronesia Media Distributor, Inc. for Micronesia; by Chips Computadoras S.A. de C.V. for Mexico; by Editorial Norma de Panama S.A. for Panama; by American Bookshops for Finland.

For general information on IDG Books Worldwide's books in the U.S., please call our Consumer Customer Service department at 800-762-2974. For reseller information, including discounts and premium sales, please call our Reseller Customer Service department at 800-434-3422.

For information on where to purchase IDG Books Worldwide's books outside the U.S., please contact our International Sales department at 317-596-5530 or fax 317-572-4002.

For consumer information on foreign language translations, please contact our Customer Service department at 1-800-434-3422, fax 317-572-4002, or e-mail rights@idgbooks.com.

For information on licensing foreign or domestic rights, please phone +1-650-653-7098.

For sales inquiries and special prices for bulk quantities, please contact our Order Services department at 800-434-3422 or write to the address above.

For information on using IDG Books Worldwide's books in the classroom or for ordering examination copies, please contact our Educational Sales department at 800-434-2086 or fax 317-572-4005.

For press review copies, author interviews, or other publicity information, please contact our Public Relations department at 650-653-7000 or fax 650-653-7500.

For authorization to photocopy items for corporate, personal, or educational use, please contact Copyright Clearance Center, 222 Rosewood Drive, Danvers, MA 01923, or fax 978-750-4470.

Table of Contents

INTRODUCTION

The great majority of computers use a version of Windows, and Windows Millennium Edition — or Windows Me — is the latest version of Windows. So if you have just purchased a new computer or have recently upgraded your system, chances are good that you need to know a bit more about Windows Me and why it is important to your PC.

Windows Me is an *operating system,* which simply means that Windows Me is software that helps your computer function. Windows Me makes it possible for your computer to run programs and do something useful.

Why Do You Need This Book?

Can you answer yes to any of these questions?

- Do you need to learn about Windows Me fast?
- Don't have time to read 500 pages about your new computer?
- Want to access the Internet in record time?
- Want to customize your computer just right?

If so, then CliffsNotes *Making Microsoft Windows Me Millennium Edition Work for You* is for you!

How to Use This Book

CliffsNotes *Making Microsoft Windows Me Millennium Edition Work for You* is a fast introduction to the world of Windows Me, whether you're a first-time computer user or just new to Windows Me. I've organized the chapters in a logical progression so that you can do real things with your computer in short order. You can skip around from topic to topic if you want.

Experienced PC users can skim through the chapters and topics to learn what's new and different about Windows Me. The chapter introductions are brief and tell you whether the chapter is of particular interest to you.

Whether you're new to PCs or a veteran user, you'll appreciate the icons that identify paragraphs of particular interest.

Think of these paragraphs as the essential truths that you must remember.

Impress your friends and confound your enemies with these gems.

Be wary! You can create big problems if you ignore this advice.

Don't Miss Our Web Site

Keep up with the exciting world of computing by visiting the CliffsNotes Web site at www.cliffsnotes.com. Here's what you find:

■ Interactive tools that are fun and informative

■ Links to interesting Web sites

■ Additional resources to help you continue your learning

At www.cliffsnotes.com, you can even register for a new feature called CliffsNotes Daily, which offers you newsletters on a variety of topics, delivered right to your e-mail inbox each business day.

If you haven't yet discovered the Internet and are wondering how to get online, pick up *Getting On the Internet*, also from CliffsNotes. You'll learn just what you need to make your online connection quickly and easily. See you at www.cliffsnotes.com!

CHAPTER 1

WINDOWS ME FOR YOU

IN THIS CHAPTER

- Defining Windows Me
- Starting Windows
- Pointing and clicking
- Mastering your keyboard
- What else is there?

For all their mystery, computers are nothing more than machines. Computers need *software* — instructions that tell the computer what to do — in order to do anything. Without software, your computer has no idea how to connect to the Internet, play a game, or check the spelling in a letter you write.

Software packages also are known as *applications* and *programs*.

Every computer must have a special type of software known as an *operating system*. An operating system is the software — such as Windows Me — that enables your computer hardware and software to work together. Without an operating system, a computer doesn't know how to do anything.

When you buy software for your Windows Me computer, make certain you get software that is designed for Windows Me (or Windows 98 if Windows Me is not specifically mentioned). Software is designed for specific operating systems and generally won't function unless you have the correct one. Fortunately, Windows Me can run nearly any software designed for Windows-based PCs, so you have lots to choose from.

Starting Windows Me

You don't have to do anything special to start Windows Me other than to turn on your computer's power switch. The power switch may be on the front, side, or back of the PC cabinet. If your monitor has a separate power switch, you need to switch it on, too.

If your PC was turned off, it may take a few moments for Windows Me to load and make your computer ready to use.

As Windows Me loads, you will eventually see the desktop with a number of program icons, the Start button, and an hourglass in the middle of your screen. As soon as the hourglass goes away, you can begin using your computer.

Because Windows Me has a *graphical user interface*, or GUI (pronounced "gooey"), you work with your computer by using on-screen icons and menus. This means that you can use your mouse and your keyboard to select the program or document that you want to use instead of trying to remember some esoteric instruction. GUIs make computers far easier to use than they were in the days when you had to type commands to do anything — for one thing, you don't have to worry about typing in the wrong command. Figure 1-1 shows a typical Windows Me screen.

Pointing and Clicking

You interact with Windows Me by using your keyboard and mouse. If you aren't yet comfortable with a mouse, you may be trying to avoid using it as much as possible. But in Windows Me, the mouse is so important that you'll find that avoiding your mouse makes life much more difficult.

Figure 1-1:   The Windows Me desktop is the way you interact with your PC.

The important Windows desktop features are covered in this book. Table 1-1 shows where to look in the book.

Table 1-1:   Windows Desktop

Feature	Location
Start button	Chapter 2
Taskbar	Chapter 2
Taskbar button	Chapter 2
System Tray	Chapter 5
Recycle Bin	Chapter 6

Even if moving the mouse around and clicking things seems awkward at first, you'll soon discover that your mouse and Windows Me were made for each other.

Moving the pointer on the screen

The on-screen — or mouse — pointer moves in the same direction as your mouse. If you move the mouse forward, the pointer moves up. If you move left or right, the pointer also moves left or right. If the mouse isn't moving in the correct direction, you are probably not holding the mouse correctly. If your mouse has a cord, the cord should stick out away from you as you face your desk.

Your PC might use an alternate means of moving the pointer, such as a touch pad, a roller ball, or a pointing stick. Use these alternative pointing devices in these ways:

■ The base of a roller ball stays in one place, and you roll the ball in the direction in which you want the pointer to move.

■ A pointing stick doesn't actually move, but it does sense the pressure that you apply and moves the pointer in the direction in which you apply pressure.

■ Slide one finger across a touch pad in the direction in which you want the pointer to move. Never use a pen or any other type of device on a touch pad and avoid allowing more than one finger to touch the pad — this confuses your system and may cause the pointer to jump erratically. Be careful not to tap on the touch pad because this is usually interpreted as clicking the left mouse button.

If your laptop PC has both a touch pad and a pointing stick, you'll probably find that only one of them can be active. Pressing certain key combinations that are specific to your brand of PC generally does switching between the two.

Clicking the buttons

New users often experience a certain amount of confusion about using the mouse buttons. Sometimes you need a single-click, and sometimes you need a double-click — which means that you must quickly click the button twice in a row. Sometimes you use the left button, and sometimes the right one.

Generally, though, you can safely assume certain things about mouse clicks:

■   A single-click opens a menu or activates a command that appears on a program's menu. Menus never require a double-click.

■   If the names under desktop icons are underlined, a single-click activates the object that is associated with the icon. You can tell that an icon has been activated if the pointer changes to an hourglass.

■   If the icon names are not underlined, a single-click usually just selects the icon. In this case, you need to double-click to activate it.

■   By default, the left mouse button selects or activates items. When someone tells you to click or double-click an object, they usually mean that you should use the left button.

■   The right mouse button generally displays a *context sensitive menu* for an item, which means that the menu lists only actions that you can perform on the selected object. Right-click menus change according to the type of object you select.

■   Windows Explorer — a program you use to see the files on your computer — uses the same number of clicks as the desktop icons, so if you use a single-click to activate desktop icons, you also use single-clicks to open items in Windows Explorer.

Some mice have a third button or even a small wheel between the buttons. The function of the third button varies depending on the type of mouse and the application that you're using. The small wheel is typically used for *scrolling* — moving up and down on a page that is displayed on your screen.

Dragging and dropping

You can use your mouse to easily copy or move objects by using a technique known as *drag and drop*. You select an object and then use your mouse to drag it to the desired destination. As you drag the object, you hold down the left mouse button and release it only when the mouse pointer is pointing to the location where you want to drop the object.

Use these special techniques with drag and drop:

- To move an object to a new location on the same disk drive, select the object, hold down the left mouse button to drag it to a new location, and drop it by releasing the button.

- To move an object to a new location on a different disk drive, hold down the Shift key while you drag and drop it.

- To copy an object to a location on the same disk drive, select the object, hold down the Ctrl key while you hold down the left mouse button to drag it to a new location, and then drop it by releasing the button.

- To copy an object to a location on a different disk drive, select the object, hold down the left mouse button to drag it to a new location, and drop it by releasing the button.

You can also drag and drop objects to and from documents. You must, however, drop the object onto the correct application window — you can't drop objects onto the taskbar buttons. If you can't see the destination window, move the mouse pointer over the taskbar button, continue to hold down the left mouse button, and then drag the object into the window when it opens.

If you want to drag and drop multiple items, select all the items before you begin to drag them to a new location. You can select a contiguous range of items by selecting the first item in the list, holding down the Shift key, and moving the mouse pointer to select the final item. You can select items that are not adjacent by holding down the Ctrl key as you click each item.

Adjusting your mouse

You can swap the functions of the mouse buttons, change the response time for clicking, or make the pointer move at a different rate with just a few quick adjustments. To adjust your mouse settings, follow these steps:

1. Choose Start⇨Settings⇨Control Panel. The Control Panel window appears.

2. Click (or double-click) the Mouse icon to open the Mouse Properties dialog box. You may need to click the View all Control Panel Options item to see this icon.

3. To swap the functions of the right and left mouse buttons, choose the button configuration option that you prefer.

4. To make the mouse respond to your double-clicks, drag the Double-click Speed slider left or right and then double-click in the Test Area box.

5. Click the Motion tab to adjust the speed at which the mouse pointer moves and whether you want a pointer trail (which makes it easier to see the mouse pointer).

6. Click OK to close the dialog box and apply your changes.

Mastering Your Keyboard

Your keyboard is also very important in Windows Me. You use your keyboard to enter information into nearly every type of document you work with.

Pressing special keys

You can use many keyboard shortcuts in Windows Me. Table 1-2 shows the more popular shortcuts that can save you lots of time. In the table, a plus sign (+) means that you hold down the first key as you press the second key.

Table 1-2: Important Windows Me Keyboard Shortcuts

Action	Shortcut
Activate a selected object	Enter
Cancel a menu or dialog box	Esc
Close the current program	Alt+F4
Copy the selected object	Ctrl+C
Cut the selected object	Ctrl+X
Delete the selected object	Delete
Display the Start menu	Ctrl+Esc (or Windows key)
Open a Help window	F1
Paste an object that you cut or copied	Ctrl+V
Refresh the view	F5
Rename an item	F2
Select all items	Ctrl+A
Undo an action	Ctrl+Z

Adjusting your keyboard

Just as your mouse may need some adjustment to be as comfortable as possible, your keyboard may need some tuning up, too. Use these steps to adjust your PC keyboard to make typing easier:

1. Choose Start⇨Settings⇨Control Panel.

2. Click (or double-click) the Keyboard icon to open the Keyboard Properties dialog box.

3. To set the amount of time a key must be held down before it begins repeating, drag the Repeat Delay slider left for a long delay or right for a shorter delay.

4. Drag the Repeat Rate slider left or right to adjust how quickly the same character repeats when a key is held down.

5. Drag the Cursor Blink Rate slider to adjust the frequency of the flashing of the cursor.

6. Click OK to confirm your changes and close the dialog box.

What Else Is There?

Warning

You've probably heard about some of the other operating systems, such as Linux, BeOS, and the Mac OS. Although these alternatives are made for certain types of PCs, none of them is compatible with Windows Me. Any programs that you run on your Windows Me system must be specifically designed for Windows Me (or at least Windows-based PCs). Programs designed for other operating systems won't work on your Windows Me PC. Nor, for that matter, will your Windows Me applications run on those other operating systems.

Some other members of the Windows family are quite compatible with Windows Me. Windows 98 (the predecessor to Windows Me) is quite similar to Windows Me and is still in use on lots of PCs. Windows 2000 and its predecessor, Windows NT 4, are also similar to Windows Me. Most programs that run on Windows Me also run on Windows 98 and Windows 2000. To run efficiently, Windows 2000 requires a more powerful PC than is necessary for Windows Me.

CHAPTER 2

GET YOUR PROGRAMS RUNNING (HEAD OUT ON THE HIGHWAY. . .)

IN THIS CHAPTER

- Defining programs
- Opening and starting programs
- Switching between programs
- Closing programs

Programs are what make your PC useful. In this chapter, you learn the essentials of running programs on your Windows Me PC.

What Are Programs?

Programs — commonly known as *applications* — are the pieces of software that make your computer perform specific tasks. Computers are flexible machines that use programs to enable them to perform many different functions. For example, these popular programs can help you make your Windows Me PC do some very different things:

- *Microsoft Word, Corel WordPerfect,* and *Lotus WordPro* enable your PC to function as a word processor.

- *Microsoft Excel, Corel Quattro Pro,* and *Lotus 1-2-3* enable your PC to function as a highly advanced electronic spreadsheet.

- *Quicken* and *Microsoft Money* enable your PC to help you keep track of your finances.

- *Internet Explorer, Netscape Navigator,* and *Opera* enable your PC to function as a tool for navigating and viewing the millions of pages of information on the Internet.

- *Microsoft Flight Simulator, Quake,* and *Myst* enable your PC to run games with exciting video and sounds.

Of course, these are just a few examples of the thousands of different programs that you can run on your PC.

Anything you create on your PC is considered to be a *document* — no matter whether it is a letter in a word processor or an image from your digital camera. Windows Me remembers which program you used to create each of your documents, and it uses this information to enable you to open a document directly without first opening the appropriate application program. Windows Me opens the correct program for you.

Although Windows Me automatically opens the correct program when you open a document, you still need to open the appropriate program to create new documents. In the following sections, you see several different methods for doing just that. You can choose the method that's most convenient for you.

Opening and Starting Programs

In order to use any of your programs, they must first be loaded into the computer's memory from the disk on which they are stored. You can do this in one of several ways, but typically you point and click with your mouse or select an item by using your keyboard. Often, you can choose the method that you prefer.

Starting with the Start button

At the lower-left corner of your Windows Me desktop, you see a button labeled Start — not surprisingly, this button is called the *Start button*. Clicking the Start button pops up the *Start menu* — a menu that contains entries for many of the programs that are installed on your PC. Figure 2-1 shows how the Start menu appears when you click the Start button.

You can activate the Start button and display the Start menu in several ways:

■ Move the mouse pointer over the Start button, and click the left mouse button once.

■ Hold down the Ctrl key and press the Esc key at the same time.

■ If your keyboard has a Windows key — a key with the wavy Windows flag — press it.

Figure 2-1:   Click the Start button to open the Start menu.

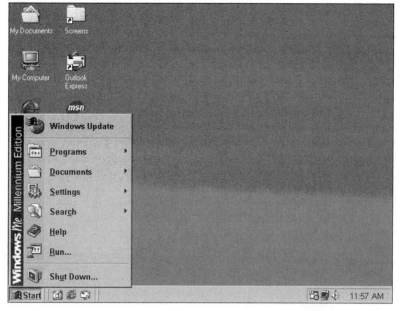

You can use the Start button even if it is hidden. Either of the keyboard methods will always display the Start menu, or you can generally make the taskbar — the bar that contains the Start button — appear by moving the mouse pointer just below the bottom edge of the screen. The mouse may not always work, however, because the taskbar may be hidden along one of the other edges of the screen, or a program may simply be preventing the mouse from displaying the taskbar.

Notice that many items on the Start menu have a small right-pointing triangle to the right of the item. This triangle indicates that another menu appears when you move the mouse pointer over the item. Slide the mouse over the second menu and then over the name of the program you want to run. When the correct program is highlighted, click the left mouse button once to run the program. Some menus may contain additional menus, so you may have to dig several levels deep to find what you want.

Starting with desktop icons

Those little pictures on your Windows Me desktop are *icons*, and they represent different programs and documents that are available on your PC. You can use these icons to open the associated programs or documents.

Your PC may be configured to open items using a single mouse click or using a double-click. To find out which method works on your computer, move the mouse pointer over one of the icons on the desktop and click the left mouse button once. Watch what happens:

■   If the mouse pointer changes to an hourglass and the program or document opens, you can open items on the desktop using a single-click.

■ If the mouse pointer does not change, the item does not open, and the name below the icon becomes highlighted, you must use a double-click to open items on the desktop. A *double-click* is two very quick, consecutive clicks of the left mouse button.

■ If nothing happens, move the mouse pointer slightly to make certain that it's actually over the icon, and then try again. Placing the pointer incorrectly at first is easy to do. With practice, you'll get it.

Starting with Windows Explorer

Your Windows Me desktop and the Start menu are somewhat limited and probably don't have entries for everything that you might want to open. To find all those other things, you will probably turn to *Windows Explorer* — a program that enables you to view all your folders and files. Figure 2-2 shows Windows Explorer as it appears on a typical PC.

To open Windows Explorer, click the Start button to open the Start menu. Then move the pointer up to open the Programs menu, over to open the Accessories menu, and finally click Windows Explorer.

Finding and opening an item that appears in Windows Explorer takes a combination of techniques that are similar to those you use on the Start menu and your desktop. Opening Windows Explorer items requires the same number of mouse clicks as opening items on your desktop. If you have to double-click to open items on the desktop, you must also double-click to open items in Windows Explorer.

You learn more about using Windows Explorer in Chapter 6.

Figure 2-2:   Use Windows Explorer to open items anywhere on your PC.

Starting with the Run dialog box

Most of the time, you will simply point and click to open things in Windows Me. But you can still type commands if necessary. You can do this one of two ways in Windows Me. The method you use depends on what you're trying to accomplish. If you simply want to start a program — such as an installation program on a CD-ROM — you can use the Run dialog box. This is a small box that appears when you click the Start button and then select Run.

You can also type certain commands at the MS-DOS Prompt, which you can find on the Programs⇨Accessories menu. Don't use the MS-DOS Prompt unless you know what you're doing or are being assisted by someone else who knows what he or she is doing.

Switching between Programs

If you want to do more than one thing with your PC, you can run different programs at the same time and then switch between them as needed. You don't have to close one program in order to use a different one.

To run more than one program at the same time, simply use your favorite method — the Start menu, the desktop icons, or whatever — to open each program. Then click the appropriate taskbar button to switch to a different program. Figure 2-3 shows how the Windows Me taskbar appears when three different programs are running at the same time.

Figure 2-3: Switch between open programs by clicking the taskbar buttons.

You can also use your keyboard to switch between open programs. First hold down the Alt key and then press the Tab key to display a box that shows icons for the programs that are currently open. Press the Tab key again and the next program in the list will be highlighted. When the program you want is selected, release the Alt key to switch to that program. If you have many programs open, you may find that using the Alt+Tab key combination is a little easier than clicking the correct taskbar button.

Closing Programs

When you're finished using a program, you should close it. This frees up some of your computer's memory for other programs, and makes certain that you don't lose any of your work.

Programs generally have an Exit (or Close) command on the File menu. If you click the File item on the program's menu bar, the File menu opens and you can scroll down to select Exit.

Warning

If you haven't saved your work when you choose File⇨Exit, you'll probably see a message asking if you want to save your changes, discard those changes, or cancel and return to the program. Each program displays a slightly different message, but you should be careful not to ignore the message because you can lose any work you've done since you last saved the document.

In addition to the File⇨Exit command, Windows Me programs also have a Close button in the upper-right corner of the program window. This button has the X in it. Clicking the Close button is the equivalent of selecting File⇨Exit or File⇨Close.

CHAPTER 3
SURF'S UP, GET ON THE WEB

IN THIS CHAPTER

- Understanding the Internet
- Understanding what you need
- Setting up your account
- Going online
- Visiting Web sites
- Playing Internet games
- Finding things online
- Communicating with MSN Messenger

The Internet is certainly the biggest news in the world of computers. These days, avoiding or ignoring the Internet is almost impossible. This chapter provides you with some Internet basics so you can begin exploring the broad range of possibilities that it holds.

Understanding the Internet

The Internet is kind of a loose connection of millions of computers all around the globe. Unlike a standard computer network, the Internet is constantly changing as people connect to and disconnect from this massive web of computers.

An Internet history lesson

Originally, the network that has become the Internet was designed to connect United States Department of Defense computers so that communications could be maintained in the event of a nuclear war. Eventually, a number of universities joined the network so that educators and researchers could easily communicate at long distances. Now that the Internet is no longer the sole domain of that early elite, it has become a tool for the people of the world to use as they see fit.

If you had a time machine and could go back to use the Internet of the early 1990s, for example, you wouldn't even recognize it as being related to the Internet of today. The Internet didn't have graphical Web pages or links that you could click — if you wanted to do anything, you had to type in a bunch of esoteric commands and hope for the best. In fact, what most people today think of as being the Internet — the World Wide Web — didn't even exist until the mid-1990s!

The World Wide Web

The World Wide Web — generally called the Web — is the part of the Internet that virtually everyone uses today. The Web is made up of *Web pages* and *Web sites* — groups of related Web pages. Web pages are documents that are located on a computer that is connected to the Internet. These documents are connected by *links* that are really nothing more than the address of the documents. In a sense, the Internet can be called a huge interconnected library that enables anyone to be one of the content contributors.

Understanding What You Need

Getting on the Internet has become much easier in the past few years. Usually, you need a few simple things for Internet access from your home:

■   A computer or a Web terminal.

- A *Web browser* — software that displays Web pages. In Windows Me, a Web browser — Internet Explorer — is built in, but you can download and install a different browser, such as Netscape Navigator or Opera if you prefer.

- An account with an *Internet service provider*, or ISP.

- Information about your Internet account, such as your *user name*, *password*, and *e-mail address*.

- A *modem* and a phone line (or some other means of physically connecting to the Internet).

If your company doesn't have Internet access over a network, don't assume you can unplug an office telephone and connect a modem for dial-up Internet access. Some business phone systems are incompatible with standard modems. In fact, you can damage your equipment if you connect a standard modem to some business phone lines. Check with your company's phone system administrator first.

Setting Up Your Account

You'll likely find that your PC already has all the hardware and software you need. Before you can connect, though, you need to set up an account with an ISP.

Finding an ISP

The first thing you must do is to choose your ISP. When choosing an ISP, consider these things:

- Make certain that you don't have to place a long distance call to connect to the Internet. Long distance charges can add up quickly!

- If you want a high-speed connection, you may find your choices limited to a few ISPs that offer DSL or cable-modem access in your area.

- Consider whether you'll ever want to access the Internet when traveling. A local ISP may offer advantages, but you won't be able to access your e-mail without making a long distance call if you're on a trip out of your local area.

- You should ask other people in your area which ISPs they use and whether they're satisfied. If everyone is complaining about a particular ISP, you may want to avoid that one.

You can probably find at least one ISP in the Yellow Pages listed under the Internet category. You can also find out which national ISPs serve your area by using the Windows Me Internet Connection Wizard. Click the Start button and choose Programs⊏>Accessories⊏>Communications⊏>Internet Connection Wizard to start the Wizard.

National ISPs often provide installation software that sets up your account automatically.

Getting your account information

Regardless of the ISP that you choose, you probably have to supply a credit card number to pay for your account — although some ISPs will bill you if you don't want to use a credit card. The ISP, in turn, should supply you with the following information:

- Your *account name* — the name that you enter when you connect to the Internet.

- Your *password* — a string of characters that prevent others from accessing your account.

- The *dial-in* telephone number if you use a modem to access the Internet. If the ISP has alternate numbers, you want them, too, so that your PC can try a different number if the main line is busy.

■ The name of the *mail server* so that you can send and receive e-mail.

■ The *technical support* telephone number so that you know where to call if you need help connecting.

Passwords may be *case sensitive* — that is, some letters must be capitals, others must be lowercase. Be sure that you know the proper way to enter your password.

The ISP may also tell you about any special settings that you may need to connect correctly.

Going Online

After you have the basics of getting onto the Internet, it's time to make that connection. The following sections show you how to connect the first time if you've decided to use the Internet Connection Wizard to set up an account, and then later how to connect after you have an active account.

Connecting the first time

If you have decided to try out one of the ISPs that the Internet Connection Wizard finds for you, use these steps to set up your account:

1. Click the Start button, and choose Programs⇨Accessories⇨Communications⇨Internet Connection Wizard.

2. Select the option called I Want to Sign Up and Configure My Computer for a New Internet Account.

3. Click the Next button.

4. Enter your telephone area code in the Area code text box, and click Next.

5. From the list that appears, choose an ISP and view the service offerings.

6. Click the Next button when you decide on an ISP to try.

7. Click the Finish button to confirm your choice. At this point, you need to provide your personal information to complete the online sign-up process.

If you decide to use a local ISP, the ISP will probably provide directions to help you set up a *dial-up networking* connection. For more help on Dial-Up Networking, see Chapter 9.

Connecting after your account is active

After you have set up your Internet account, you can begin using the Internet. You can use several methods to connect to the Internet — depending on what you want to accomplish:

■ The most straightforward method of connecting is to double-click the Internet Explorer icon on your desktop or to click the Internet Explorer icon in the *Quick Launch toolbar* just to the right of the Start button.

■ With some types of accounts — notably AOL — you may need to click a different icon to connect. For AOL, you would click the AOL icon.

■ If you prefer using the Windows Me menus, open the Start menu and select Programs➪Internet Explorer.

You may need to confirm that you want to connect, so you can verify the dial-up phone number, your account name, and your password.

If you click the Remember password check box, anyone with access to your computer can connect to your Internet account without knowing your password. This may also give them access to your e-mail account.

If you use a modem that is connected to your PC, Windows Me displays a connection icon in the *system tray* next to the clock. This icon has two lights that flash green as data is sent over your phone line. The connect icon disappears when the connection is broken — providing you with a visual clue that your phone line is once again available. Normally, the connection is broken when you close Internet Explorer, but you can also break the connection manually by right-clicking the connection icon and choosing Disconnect.

Tip

You can check the current connection status by right-clicking the connection icon and choosing Status from the menu.

Visiting Web Sites

After you are connected to the Internet, the fun begins. In the following sections, you learn how to browse the Web.

Understanding Internet addresses

Each Web page has a *URL* — Uniform Resource Locator — that uniquely identifies exactly how to locate the page. A URL is really the address of a Web page, and URLs enable your Web browser to find and display the pages that you want to see. Here's a breakdown of how URLs are specified:

```
Protocol://address/subaddress1 . . .
```

The *protocol* is simply an indicator of the type of address that you want to visit. In most cases, Web pages use `http` — Hypertext Transfer Protocol (or `https` if the Web site is on a secure server, such as one that takes credit card orders). A colon and two forward slashes (`://`) always follow the protocol. Next follows the Web site address, such as `www.cliffsnotes.com`. If you want to visit a page that is part of the same Web site, that page address is indicated by a slash and then the page address. In some cases, Web pages may be several levels deep, so several slashes may separate individual sub-addresses. Figure 3-1 shows where the address `http://www.cliffsnotes.com` takes you.

Figure 3-1:   A URL is the address that takes you to a Web site.

CliffsNotes: Literature, tests, computers and Internet, finance, career: books, tools, tips ...

File   Edit   View   Favorites   Tools   Help

Back ▼ → ▼ 🐼 🗋 🏠   🔍 Search   📑 Favorites   📖 History   📑▼ 🖨 💁

Address 🗐 http://www.cliffsnotes.com/index.html   ▼ 🖉 Go   Links »

CliffsNotes   KERR SMITH IS A SMARTY PANTS. FIND

Find It Quick

[   ]

SEARCH

They Saved Your Butt in S

Who's Saving It N

Student Center

Top Do

Downloads/Books ○   The Sc

CliffsNote-A-Day ○

Lit Notes ○   Creating Your Firs

Test Prep ○   Getting on t

Computer ○   Getting

Internet ○

🗐   Internet

🏁 Start   🏕 🥖 💬   🗐 CliffsNotes: Literatu...   🖥📺📶   6:06 AM

Tip

Web site addresses can't have true spaces. If you see a Web site address that appears to have a space in the address, the space is almost always filled by an *underscore* (_).

Warning

Never enter a credit card number unless you first check to see that the Web site is using the https secure protocol — otherwise your credit card number will be sent unencrypted across the Internet. Look in the Address Bar to make certain the Web page address begins with https rather than simply http.

Using links

Most Web pages include a number of *links* that you can click to jump to other Web pages. This collection of links gives the Web its name because the links extend in all directions, almost like a spider web. Links often appear as underlined text that makes them easy to identify, but links can also be buttons or pictures. Whenever your mouse pointer is over a link, the pointer changes from an arrow to a hand.

Sometimes when you click a link, you may receive a message telling you that the address cannot be located or that the server is not responding. This can mean that the page no longer exists, or it might just be that the Web server is temporarily unavailable due to routine maintenance. You can simply wait and try the link again later.

Saving your favorite sites

You will probably find that some Web pages quickly become favorite sites that you visit again and again. To make it easier to return to these sites, you can save the URLs in your list of favorite Web sites. Then you can quickly return to a site by clicking a link in your Favorites list.

To add a site to your list of favorites, choose Favorites⇨ Add to Favorites to display the Add Favorite dialog box, as shown in Figure 3-2. You can also right-click the current Web page and choose Add to Favorites from the pop-up context menu to save the page to your favorites list. You may want to modify the default name that Internet Explorer offers for the site to make the name more descriptive.

Use folders to help organize your favorites. When the Add Favorite dialog box is open, click the Create In button to expand the dialog box. Then choose one of the existing folders or click the New Folder button and create a folder.

After you have saved your favorite Web site addresses, click the Favorites menu and choose the site from the list to return to that site.

Figure 3-2:   Save your favorite Web page addresses so you can easily return to those pages.

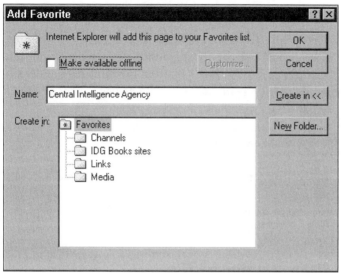

Using the Address toolbar

If you want Internet Explorer to go directly to a particular Web page, you can type the URL in the Internet Explorer Address box. If Internet Explorer is not currently open, you can open an address box on the Windows Me Taskbar by following these steps:

1. Right-click the Windows Me taskbar.

2. Choose Toolbars⇨Address from the pop-up context menu.

3. Type the URL in the Address box and press Enter.

When you press Enter, Internet Explorer loads, makes the connection to the Internet, and goes directly to the page you specify.

Sending links and pages

If you find an interesting Web page that you'd like to share, you can easily send a link or a whole Web page to someone via e-mail. To simply send a link to the page, choose File⇨Send⇨Link by E-mail, and the message recipient can visit the page by clicking the link in your message. If you would rather send the entire Web page, choose File⇨Send⇨Page by E-mail. The Web page then appears as part of your message and the recipient can view the page as soon as she opens your message.

If you send only a link, you should include a brief message telling the recipient why she may find the Web site interesting. Many people ignore links that come with no explanation of the link.

Using the History list

Internet Explorer maintains a *History list* that contains a link to each page that you have visited. If you want to return to a particular Web page but didn't save it in your Favorites list, you can use the History list to locate the URL for the page.

The History list is organized by date and by Web site. To use the History list, you first choose the date, then the Web site, and finally the particular page on the site. When you click the link, Internet Explorer reloads the appropriate Web page.

You can set the number of days that items remain in your History list by choosing Tools⇨Internet Options. Then use the History options near the bottom of the General tab to set the number of days or to clear the History list.

You can view the History list by clicking the History button or by selecting View⇨Explorer Bar⇨History. Figure 3-3 shows how your History list might look if you visit several pages at different Web sites in a day.

Figure 3-3:   Use the History list to return to Web sites that you have visited.

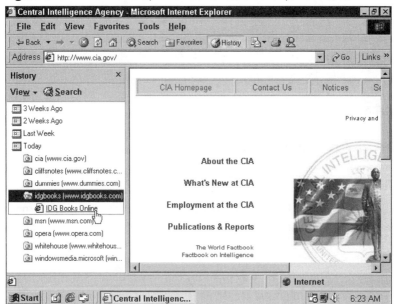

Printing Web pages

If you want to keep a permanent record of a Web page, one way to do so is to print a copy of the page. To do so, you can simply choose File➪Print, but this may not always produce the results that you really want. Consider these options:

■ All Web pages appear to Windows Me as a single page, no matter how many sheets of paper are required to print the page. To selectively choose a portion of the page to print, highlight the part you want to print before you select the File➪Print command. Make certain that the Selection radio button is selected before you click OK to begin printing.

■ To print all the pages on a Web site, select the Print All Linked Documents check box in the Print dialog box. Use this option with care — some sites can include hundreds of pages!

■ To print a list of the links on a page, select the Print Table of Links check box. This can be especially effective if you select a small portion of the page, because you can then have a printout that primarily shows the links.

You can also use the File⇨Save As command to save a Web page on your hard disk.

Finding Things Online

One of the problems you will quickly encounter on the Web is simply that it is so big that it can be overwhelming. You will need some help finding what you want on the Internet, and that help comes from *search engines* — Web services that enable you to search for specific topics of interest.

The quickest way to access the search engines is to click the Search button in Internet Explorer. This adds the Search Bar in the left pane and displays Web pages in the right pane. Then enter your search phrase in the Search the Web For text box and click Search. After you have a list of search results, click a link to view the page. Figure 3-4 shows how this works when you enter **IDG Books** as the search phrase.

Figure 3-4:   Use the Internet Explorer Search Bar to find what you want on the
Internet.

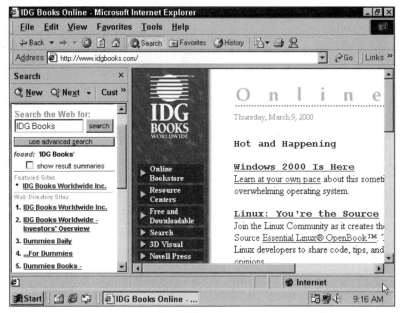

Playing Internet Games

If you like to play games but get bored having your computer
as your opponent, why not play some games on the Internet?
Windows Me includes five different games that you play
against other people via the Internet.

To play the Internet games, follow these steps:

1. Click the Start button.

2. Select Programs⇨Games, and then choose the Internet
game that you want to play.

3. Confirm that you want to connect to the MSN Gaming
Zone.

4. After you have been assigned an opponent, begin playing.

During an Internet game, you can use the Chat List box to send messages to your opponent. To send a message, choose the message from the Chat List box and click Send. When you first start participating in Internet games, you will be paired with other beginning players. As your experience level increases, you will be matched with other more experienced players.

Communicating with MSN Messenger

MSN Messenger is an *instant messaging* service that enables you to see when your friends are online and to exchange messages with them as you both surf the Internet. To use MSN Messenger, you and your friends must sign up for an MSN Passport account. But the service is free, and it takes only a few minutes to sign up.

To begin using MSN Messenger, follow these steps:

1. Click the Start button.

2. Choose Programs⇨Accessories⇨Communications⇨ MSN Messenger Service.

3. If you don't already have your MSN Passport, follow the steps to set up an account — you will have to do this only one time.

4. After you are connected, use the Add button to add new people to your list of contacts.

5. To send a message, select from your list of contacts someone who is currently online and click the Send button to open the message box. Figure 3-5 shows how this works.

Figure 3-5:   Use MSN Messenger for immediate online communications.

MSN Messenger Service ▢◻✕	ThirdOf5@passport.com - Inst... ▢◻✕
File View Tools Help	File Edit View Help

MSN Messenger window contents:

Add   Send   Status   Mail

Contacts Currently Online
  ThirdOf5@passport.com
Contacts Not Online
  DavidDavid
  Keith

• When your boss makes a mista
• Start a stock portfolio
• You are what you read

---Type a Web Search---   Search

 BrianU (Online)

Instant message window contents:

 ▾Invite   Block   Add to Contacts

To: ThirdOf5@passport.com

REMINDER: Never give out your password
or credit card number in an instant
message conversation.
BrianU says:
  Hi David;

Send

To add someone to your contact list, you must know his
MSN Passport login name. You may want to send your
friends your MSN Passport login name in an e-mail message
and ask them to send you a message with their login names.

CHAPTER 4

LIGHTS, CAMERA, ACTION!

Nothing else seems to add so much fun to computers as the sights and sounds that we call *multimedia*. In this chapter, you not only learn the basics of using these multimedia capabilities, but you also get a taste of creating your own multimedia content.

Multimedia in a Nutshell

A number of different types of things can be considered multimedia, but most people think of sounds and video. Windows Me has the ability to use several different types of multimedia files.

Understanding sound

Sound files are document files that tell your PC how to generate various types of sounds. Windows Me primarily uses two types of sound files:

- *WAV files* are recorded sounds. These sounds can include any type of sound that you can record — music, voices, sound effects, and so on. WAV files get their name from their most common file extension, .wav.

- *MIDI files* are instructions that tell your computer how to generate sounds. MIDI stands for *Musical Instrument Digital Interface*. MIDI files typically have a .mid file extension.

WAV files sound pretty much the same on any computer, but MIDI files can sound quite different because your PC is generating the sounds rather than simply playing back a recording. WAV files are also easy to create on any PC, but MIDI files require special hardware and software not found on most PCs.

Understanding video

Video files are typically document files that contain a recorded video portion along with a synchronized audio portion.

In most cases, video files that are intended for playback on a PC are best displayed in a relatively small window rather than full-screen. Some types of video files — notably MPEG files — use *data compression* to pack more multimedia content into a given amount of space.

If you have the capability to capture video into a file on your PC, you can use Movie Maker to create your own video files in Windows Media Player format. See "Making Videos with Movie Maker," later in this chapter, for more information.

Running Multimedia Files

Windows Me includes everything you need to play back a broad range of multimedia files, so you generally don't need extra software to play most multimedia content.

Playing computer sounds and videos

Windows Me use the Media Player to play back most multimedia files. Figure 4-1 shows the Media Player playing a movie file.

Figure 4-1: The Media Player plays most types of multimedia content.

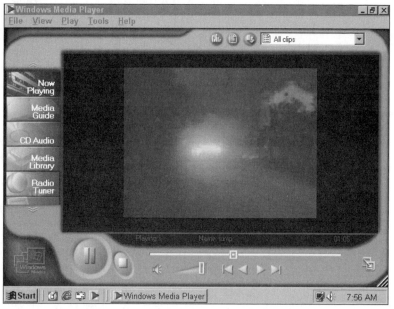

Playing a multimedia file by using the Media Player is quite easy. You have several ways to do so:

■ You can open the Start menu, choose Programs⇨ Accessories⇨Entertainment⇨Windows Media Player, and then choose File⇨Open to select files to play.

■ If the Windows Media Player is already open, you can drag and drop multimedia files onto the Windows Media Player window to play those files.

■ You can double-click a multimedia file in Windows Explorer or on your desktop to open the file and play it using Windows Media Player — Windows Me automatically opens Media Player.

Listening to music CDs

Your PC's CD-ROM drive makes a perfectly good audio CD player and even offers some advantages over most standalone CD players.

When you insert an audio CD into your CD-ROM drive, Windows Me automatically opens the Windows Media Player program. This program includes all the controls that you would normally find on a CD Player and a fun display that changes along with the music. In addition, the Windows Me Media Player can download information about your audio CDs from the Internet and can display the name of the artist, the CD name, and track information as it plays the CD.

In addition to the standard playback controls and the CD information display, the Windows Me Media Player allows you to create your own play lists for your favorite CDs. Click the Create Playlist button to edit the way the CD tracks are played. After you create a custom play list, Media Player remembers your preferences and uses the same play list the next time you insert the same audio CD.

Making Sounds Automatic

In some cases, you may want Windows Me to play sounds automatically to provide you with audio clues that certain things have happened. In this section, you learn how to add the sounds you want.

Windows Me keeps a list of *system events* — things that happen on your computer — that can have sounds associated with them. These are the events for which you can choose to add recorded sounds — WAV files. As you learn later in this chapter, in the section "Recording Your Own Sounds," you can even create your own sounds to add to events.

To add sounds to system events, follow these steps:

1. Choose Start⇨Settings⇨Control Panel.

2. Double-click the Sounds and Multimedia icon in the Control Panel to open the Sounds and Multimedia Properties dialog box, as shown in Figure 4-2.

Figure 4-2:   Add your own sounds to Windows Me events.

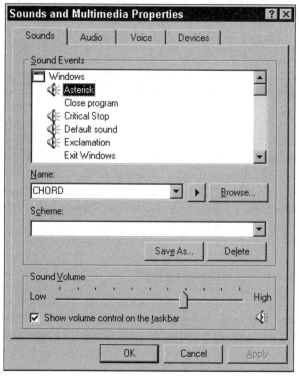

3. Click one of the events that has a sound — look for the speaker icon in front of events with sounds — and click the Play button.

4. Select an event, and click the Browse button to look for a sound file to attach to the event.

5. Click OK to return to the Sounds and Multimedia Properties dialog box.

6. If you want to save different sound schemes, use the Save As button to name each scheme.

7. Click OK to close the dialog box.

You can also add sounds to your documents. If you find an Insert menu in a program, use the Insert⇨File command to add a sound file to the document. You can also use the drag-and-drop technique (discussed in Chapter 1) to add a sound file to most documents.

Controlling the Volume

The sounds you play on your PC are of no use if they're too quiet, and they're no fun if they're too loud. You may need to use the Windows Me volume control to adjust the volume level so that it's just right.

Adjusting volume

Windows Me has a master volume control in the *system tray* next to the time display in the Windows Me taskbar. The volume control icon looks like a speaker.

To adjust the overall volume level, click the volume control icon, which displays a slider that you can drag up or down to adjust the volume.

If you need to quickly disable all sounds — perhaps to answer a phone call — click the volume icon once and then select the Mute check box.

Balancing sound sources

You have probably noticed that some sounds play louder than others. Your WAV sounds might be too loud, but your audio

CDs might be too soft. You can balance the various sound sources using the full volume control that has individual sliders for each sound source. The full volume control also has balance sliders to adjust the right/left speaker balance.

To display the full volume control, double-click the system tray speaker icon. Use the separate controls to adjust each sound source for an optimum mix. You find a Select check box for each sound source so that you can silence any one source individually by clicking to remove the check from its check box.

Customizing the volume control panel

The controls that appear on the full volume control are generally the ones that are most important for playing back sounds. You can add or remove individual controls by choosing Options⇨Properties and then clicking the check box for the controls you want to see. You might want to see different controls to adjust the levels for recording.

Recording Your Own Sounds

You can create your own WAV files by recording sounds that play through your PC's sound card. You can, for example, record voice messages to send along with an e-mail message, or a special message to advise you of a Windows Me system event. You need a microphone to record a voice message.

Although you can record sounds from virtually any sound source, remember that commercially produced materials are covered by copyrights.

Using the Sound Recorder

You can record your own sound files using the *Sound Recorder* — a Windows Me accessory.

Before you begin recording, open the full volume control and make certain that the microphone input is not muted. Otherwise, your message won't be recorded.

To record a message, click the Start button and then select Programs⇨Accessories⇨Entertainment⇨Sound Recorder. Next, click the Record button and begin speaking. The small window in the center of the Sound Recorder shows the differences in volume level, so if the line stays flat, it's a good indication that your sound source may not be properly enabled (or that the volume is simply set too low). After you finish recording, click the Stop button. Then use the buttons and the slider to play back the recording. Choose File⇨Save to keep your recording.

Setting the sound properties

You can choose different quality levels for your recordings, depending on whether you want higher quality or smaller sound files. Higher quality levels generally use considerably more disk space. To choose the recording quality level, follow these steps in Sound Recorder:

1. Choose File⇨Properties.

2. Click the Convert Now button.

3. Choose the quality level that you prefer. Notice that each quality level provides an indication of the size of the sound file.

4. Close the dialog boxes, and return to Sound Recorder to use the new settings for your next recording.

Making Videos with Movie Maker

Windows Me includes a tool called Movie Maker that you can use to create your own video productions. Movie Maker creates videos in a format that can be played in Media Player, so you can distribute your videos to anyone who uses Windows. To open Movie Maker, click the Start button and choose Programs⇨Accessories⇨Entertainment⇨Windows Movie Maker.

Opening videos

You can open existing video files or record your own videos directly into Movie Maker. To open an existing video file, select File⇨Import and choose the file that you want to open. To record a new video, choose File⇨Record.

Your PC must be equipped with a video capture device if you want to record your own videos. Some video adapters include a video capture port that can accept a signal from a video source such as a camcorder or VCR. Digital camcorders can usually save video files in a format that Movie Maker can import.

When you open a video file, Movie Maker automatically breaks the file into *clips* — roughly the equivalent of scenes. This may take a few minutes when you first open the file.

Arranging your story line

After your video file is broken into clips, you can begin to assemble the clips into a story line. This simply means that you arrange the individual scenes in the order in which you want them to appear in your completed movie. Movie Maker provides a *storyboard* that you use to assemble your movie by dragging and dropping clips onto the storyboard. Figure 4-3 shows how the storyboard appears after several clips have been dropped in the desired sequence.

You can click the Play button to view the current layout of your movie. If you click one of the clips in the storyboard, Movie Maker plays the current movie starting with the selected clip.

Figure 4-3: Drag and drop the clips onto the storyboard to assemble your movie.

![Windows Movie Maker screenshot showing the clip thumbnail pane with Clip 1, Clip 2, Clip 3, and Clip 4, a preview pane, playback controls, and a storyboard along the bottom.]

To play a single clip, select the clip in the clip thumbnail pane and then click Play.

If you want to add a narration track to your assembled movie, click the Add Narration icon to the left of the storyboard and then record your narration. A narration track can include music in addition to vocal narration.

Saving your movie

After you have assembled your movie and added any sounds that you want played with the video, choose File⇨Save Movie to display the Save Movie dialog box. Choose the quality level (remembering that higher quality means larger file sizes), enter the Media Player information, and click OK. Enter a name for the video file and choose the proper location before you click the Save button.

Movie Maker movie files have an .asf file extension — short for Advanced Streaming Format — which Windows Me automatically associates with the Media Player.

CHAPTER 5

BRINGING OUT THE ME IN WINDOWS ME

- Personalizing your screen
- Arranging your desktop
- Personalizing your Start menu
- Starting screen savers

Your Windows Me PC can be as personal as you like. You can change the appearance of nearly every element of the Windows Me screen to make your desktop unique, to improve the readability, or even to project a specific corporate image.

In this chapter, you learn how to make the visual adjustments that can make any PC look just the way you like.

Personalizing Your Screen

All the Windows Me appearance settings are conveniently accessible through the Display Properties dialog box — or through dialog boxes that you open from the Display Properties dialog box. To begin making changes to the Windows Me appearance options, start by opening the Display Properties dialog box. To do so, right-click a blank area of the desktop and choose Properties from the pop-up context menu.

Keep the Display Properties dialog box open as you read through the following sections.

The Display Properties dialog box may include options specific to your display adapter that are not covered here. You can ignore those options for now.

Selecting the background image

Begin selecting the display options on the Background tab as shown in Figure 5-1. If this tab is not already in front, click it to make it the active tab.

Figure 5-1: Use the Background tab to select desktop wallpaper.

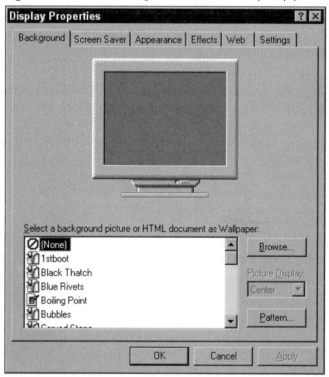

If you want to add *wallpaper* to your desktop, choose an image file from the list box or click the Browse button and select a file on your hard disk. You might, for example, choose an image created by your digital camera.

If the image you choose does not completely fill the desktop, you can select an option from the drop-down Picture Display list box. The three options enable you to center, tile, or stretch the image. You may need to experiment to see which image effect you prefer.

You can choose from several different types of image files. To display HTML documents or JPEG images, Windows Me must first activate the *Active Desktop* feature — which it offers to do if you select one of these file types.

You can also choose a repeating pattern for your desktop rather than an image. To do so, click the Pattern button and choose the pattern you prefer. If you choose both a background image and a pattern, the pattern only appears outside the edges of the background image.

Desktop wallpaper appears behind everything else on your desktop so that you can always see the desktop icons.

Click Apply to apply any changes you've made before moving from one tab to another. Keeping track of your changes is far easier if you make a few at a time.

Changing lettering

Click the Appearance tab to bring it to the front so that you can change the colors and font settings that Windows Me uses. This tab is shown in Figure 5-2.

Be sure to click the Save As button before you begin making changes so you can easily reverse any changes that you don't like.

The easiest way to change the whole set of color and font settings is to select one of the predefined schemes from the Scheme list box. Click the down arrow at the right edge of the list box to drop down the list so you can make a selection.

Figure 5-2: Use the Appearance tab to select colors and fonts.

To make individual changes yourself, click the item that you want to change in the sample area (or choose the item from the Item list box). Then use the various option boxes to make your color, size, and font choices.

You can create several different sets of color and font selections by saving your choices under new names. Click the Save As button and create a name for the new set.

Adding special effects

Click the Effects tab, shown in Figure 5-3, and you find a number of interesting options:

■ Select one of the standard desktop icons from the list box, and then click the Change Icon button if you'd like to choose your own desktop icons. Click the Default Icon button to return an icon to its original appearance.

Figure 5-3:   Use the Effects tab to select icons and some special effects.

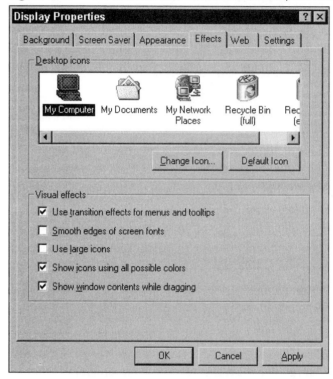

■ Select the Use Transition Effects for Menus and Tooltips check box if you want your menus to be animated.

■ Select the Smooth Edges of Screen Fonts check box to improve the appearance of text — especially in the larger sizes — that appears on your screen.

■ Select the Use Large Icons check box if you want Windows Me to use icons that are about twice the normal size on your desktop.

- Select the Show Icons Using All Possible Colors check box to make the icons as colorful as possible.

- Select the Show Window Contents While Dragging check box to show on-screen windows while they're being moved around the screen. If this option is not selected, you see only an outline of the window as you drag the window.

Sharpening the picture

Click the Settings tab, as shown in Figure 5-4, so you can adjust the number of colors that are displayed and the screen resolution.

The Colors list box enables you to choose the number of colors that can be displayed at one time. Images generally appear more lifelike when more colors are displayed, but your computer may take slightly longer to display images if the higher settings are selected.

The Screen Area slider enables you to choose the screen resolution. Higher resolution settings enable you to have more things on the screen at the same time, but they tend to make items much smaller.

The two settings on the Settings tab are interrelated. That is, if you choose a very high setting on one option, you may not be able to choose the setting you want on the other. This depends on the capabilities of your display adapter.

When you click the Apply button to change your screen resolution or number of colors, Windows Me resizes the screen and asks if you want to keep the new settings. If you don't confirm that you want to keep the new settings within 15 seconds, Windows Me restores your old settings. In a few cases, you may need to restart your computer to apply the new settings.

Figure 5-4: Use the Settings tab to select screen resolution and number of colors.

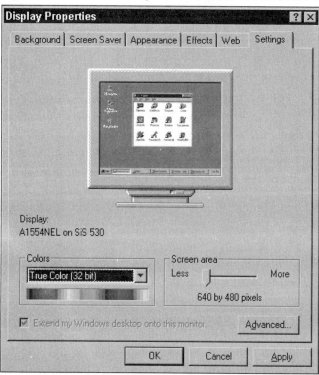

Improving picture performance

If you want to make certain that your monitor is as *flicker-free* as possible in order to reduce the possibility of eyestrain, click the Advanced button near the bottom of the Settings tab. This displays a Properties dialog box specific to your display adapter and monitor. The Properties dialog box varies according to the display adapter installed in your system, but you may see these common settings:

■ On the General tab, make certain that the Show Settings Icon on Taskbar check box is selected. This setting displays a small icon in the system tray that you can then click to choose between the available screen color depth and resolution settings.

■ On the Adapter tab, the Change button enables you to select a different display adapter. If your color depth setting is stuck at 16 colors and your resolution setting is stuck at 640x480 (VGA) or 800x600 (SVGA), you may have your adapter specified incorrectly. You should choose the correct brand and model of display adapter rather than VGA or SVGA — the less capable defaults Windows Me will use if it has not correctly identified your display adapter.

■ If the Adapter tab includes a Refresh rate setting, you may be able to reduce flicker by choosing a higher refresh rate — the number of times the image is redrawn each second. You must choose a setting that is compatible with your monitor to prevent damage to your monitor, but you should choose a setting of at least 72Hz if possible. See your monitor's user manual to see which settings you can safely use.

■ On the Monitor tab, the Change button enables you to specify the correct brand and model of your monitor.

■ The Performance tab includes a slider that you can use to adjust the level of hardware-assisted graphics acceleration that is used. Normally you should simply leave this at Full to make your PC run at its fastest level. You probably won't need to adjust this unless a tech support person wants to try a lower setting to attempt to isolate a problem.

Making your desktop look like a Web page

If you click the Web tab of the Display Properties dialog box, you can choose to view your desktop as a Web page. This enables you to use both HTML documents and JPEG image files as the background for your desktop, and it also allows you to add *active content* — such as a current weather map or stock ticker — to your desktop. To add active content, you must click the New button and visit the Microsoft Web site.

If you select an HTML document or a JPEG image as desktop wallpaper, Windows Me automatically enables the active desktop.

Arranging Your Desktop

If your Windows Me desktop is a real mess, you can bring some order to it by using a few simple options:

■ You can drag and drop icons on your desktop to rearrange them.

■ You can right-click a blank space on the desktop and choose Line Up Icons from the pop-up context menu to move the icons into orderly columns with the icons evenly spaced.

■ You can right-click a blank space on the desktop, choose Arrange Icons, and then choose a sort order to sort the icons by name, type, size, or date.

■ You can right-click a blank space on the desktop and choose Arrange Icons⇨Auto Arrange to automatically line up the icons whenever a new icon is added, an existing icon is deleted, or icons are dropped into the middle of existing icons.

If you choose to use the Auto Arrange option, you can drop icons between other icons to change the arrangement. Icons below the point you drop the new icon move down (or to the top of the next column) to make room for the new icon.

Personalizing Your Start Menu

You probably use the Windows Me Start menu quite often, so you want to make certain that it is easy to use. You can make several changes that help keep your Start menu under control. The following sections show you a number of important things you can do.

Rearranging by dragging and dropping

The quickest method of rearranging your Start menu is to drag and drop items. To move an item to a new menu location, point to the item that you want to move, hold down the left mouse button, drag it to the new location, and release the mouse button to drop the item. If you want to move something to a different menu level, drag the item onto the menu and wait for the menu to open. Move the mouse pointer to the desired destination, and drop the item.

You can also drag and drop things onto the Start menu from your desktop or from Windows Explorer.

Rearranging by exploring your Start menu

Although the drag and drop method is a convenient way to quickly rearrange a few items on your Start menu, moving a number of items isn't so easy. For this, you may want to use Windows Explorer to explore your Start menu.

Begin by right-clicking the Start button and choosing Explore from the pop-up context menu. This opens Windows Explorer with the C:\Windows\Start Menu folder open. Click the plus sign in the box to the left of the Programs folder to expand the display and then click the folder icon to display the contents of the Programs folder.

After you open the Programs folder, you can move items, create new folders, and generally rearrange the folder items as you see fit. Any changes you make are reflected in the menus when you next open the Start menu.

Warning

You should place only *shortcuts* — links to files you can click for quick access to the file — and folders within the Programs folder and its subfolders. Never place actual programs in the Programs folder or on your desktop.

Sorting your Start menu

As soon as you make manual changes to the menus, Windows Me stops doing automatic menu organization. By default, Windows Me displays items on the menus in alphabetical order, with submenus at the top of each menu. After you make a manual change to the menus, Windows Me allows items to appear in any order on the menus. The quickest method of re-sorting a menu is to open the menu, right-click the open menu, and choose Sort by Name from the pop-up context menu.

Controlling what appears on your Start menu

Although most of the rearrangement that you can do is on the Programs menu rather than on the Start menu itself, you do have some level of control over which items appear on the Start menu. To select these options, right-click the Taskbar and choose Properties from the pop-up context menu. Then click the Advanced tab on the Taskbar and Start Menu Properties dialog box and choose the items you want from the list box near the bottom of the dialog box. Click OK to make your changes.

Starting Screen Savers

Modern PCs simply don't need *screen savers*. Unlike some PCs many years ago, modern monitors do not suffer damage by having an unchanging image displayed on the screen.

Screen savers can serve one semi-useful purpose. If you specify a password, someone needs the correct password to disable the screen saver and view your desktop.

The screen saver password really offers very little protection because anyone can bypass it by turning your system off and back on.

Choosing a screen saver

If you want to use one of the screen savers to make your screen a bit more colorful when you aren't working with your system, right-click a blank space on your desktop and choose Properties from the pop-up context menu. Click the Screen Saver tab to bring it to the front, as shown in Figure 5-5.

Next, click the down arrow at the right side of the Screen Saver list box and choose an option from the list. To see a full-screen preview of the screen saver, click the Preview button.

Be careful not to move your mouse or press any keys until you finish viewing the full-screen preview because this will close the screen saver.

Customizing a screen saver

Most screen savers include a number of settings that you can play around with. Often, you can change the speed, the texture, the size, and the motion of the objects that are drawn on the screen. Screen savers that display text can generally use custom text that you specify. The settings vary according to which screen saver you select, but in each case, clicking the Settings button displays a setup dialog box for the screen saver.

Figure 5-5:   Use the Screen Saver tab to select a screen saver.

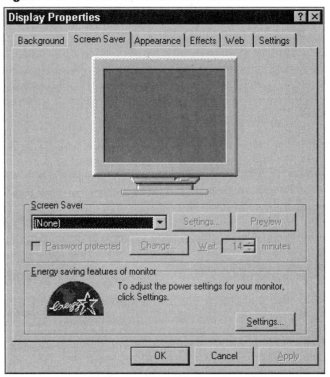

The Wait setting, which specifies how long Windows Me waits before it displays the screen saver, applies to all screen savers. The waiting time restarts whenever you press a key or move your mouse. Use the up or down arrows at the right edge of the Wait spin box to select the waiting time.

If you want to use a password, follow these steps:

1. Select (add a check to) the Password Protected check box.

2. Click the Change button to display the Change Password dialog box.

3. Enter the same password in both text boxes. The password that you type doesn't appear — asterisks are shown in place of each character.

4. Click OK to close the dialog box.

Be sure to remember your password exactly. If you forget your password, you can't close the screen saver without shutting down your system, and you won't be able to specify a new password.

CHAPTER 6

KEEPING TRACK OF YOUR PERSONAL FILES

IN THIS CHAPTER

- Using Windows Explorer
- Using disks
- Finding files

Your PC can store literally thousands of files in hundreds of different locations, and this can make finding specific files a difficult task if you don't know where and how to look for them. This task can be especially frustrating if the file you're trying to find is the document that you're sure you saved, but aren't quite sure where it ended up. In this chapter, you learn how to cut the task down to size so that you never have to worry about lost files again.

In addition to finding your files, you also want to know how to organize your files by using folders. This chapter shows you how to create and use folders, as well as how to prepare disks so that you can use them.

Using Windows Explorer

Windows Explorer is a Windows Me program that you use to view the contents of all your disk drives, as well as any resources on your network (if you have a network). You can do many things in Windows Explorer, including viewing, opening, copying, moving, deleting, and renaming files.

Looking at Windows Explorer

Windows Explorer normally displays two separate *panes* — windows within the Windows Explorer window. The left pane typically shows the *Folders Explorer Bar*. This is a structured view that shows the relationships between the disk drives and folders on your computer. The right pane — the contents pane — shows the items inside the currently selected folder. As you move around and select different folders, the contents pane shows the contents of the selected folder.

Naming folders

Folders are where you store things on your disk drives. Folders can contain files, of course, but they can also contain additional folders. For example, the following *pathname* describes the location of a folder that is five levels deep in the folder structure:

```
C:\Windows\Start
Menu\Programs\Accessories\Entertainment
```

Each separate folder name is delineated by a backslash (\). In this case the drive is C:, and the folders are Windows, Start Menu, Programs, Accessories, and Entertainment. Each later folder is inside the preceding folder. That is, the Entertainment folder is inside the Accessories folder, and so on.

In Windows Me, you can name a file with up to 255 characters, including spaces. Filenames can't contain the characters \ / : * ? " < > | and must be unique within a folder. You can have two files with the same basic name only if they are in separate folders. Windows Me warns you if you try to assign identical names to two files in the same folder.

Managing files

To open Windows Explorer, click the Start button and then choose Programs⇨Accessories⇨Windows Explorer. This

opens the Windows Explorer window with disk drive C:
selected. To select a different drive or folder, click the drive
or folder in the Folders Explorer Bar.

Folders have a horizontal line to their left that connects to
the vertical line. The vertical line extends down from a drive
or folder icon to connect to all the folders contained within
the drive or folder. Some folders have a small box where the
horizontal line connects to the vertical line that tells you that
the folder with the box contains additional folders. If the box
contains a plus sign (+), those additional folders are not currently being displayed — the folder display is *collapsed*. A
minus sign (-) indicates that the folder has been *expanded* to
show the additional folders it contains. You can click the box
to expand or collapse the display.

To select a folder to show in the contents pane, click the
folder's icon. An open folder icon indicates the currently
selected folder, while all other folders have a closed folder
icon. Figure 6-1 shows how the Folders Explorer Bar appears
when some folders are expanded, some are collapsed, and one
folder is open.

After you open a folder using the Folders Explorer Bar, you
can switch over to the contents pane to work with individual files. To open a file, you can simply double-click the file
(single-click if you have configured your system for single-
clicks). You can do these additional things:

- ■ Use the drag-and-drop techniques you learned in
  Chapter 1 to copy or move files to new locations.

- ■ Right-click a file to display a context-sensitive menu
  showing actions that you can perform on the file (see
  Figure 6-2). This menu varies depending on the type of
  file you select.

Figure 6-1: Use the Folders Explorer bar to navigate your folders.

Figure 6-2: Right-click an item to open a context-sensitive menu.

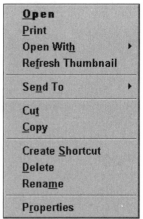

■ Right-click a file and choose Send To⇨3½ Floppy (A) to save a copy of the file on a removable disk in drive A:. Don't try this with very large files because removable disks have limited space.

- Select a file and press the Delete key to send the file to the Windows Me Recycle Bin. In Chapter 7, you learn how to work with the Recycle Bin so you can recover files that you accidentally delete.

- Select a file and press the F2 key if you want to rename the file. If the filename shows an *extension* — one to three characters following a period at the end of the name — make certain that you don't change the extension. Changing the extension can cause problems when Windows Me tries to open files.

Be especially careful in deleting, moving, or renaming files. Unless the file is one that you created, you can cause severe problems by doing any of these things to unknown files. In extreme cases, you may cause some programs to fail or possibly even prevent Windows Me itself from running.

Viewing folders

You have several different choices on how the contents pane shows the items in each folder. You can change the display so that it shows the largest number of icons in the smallest space, or you may want to see as many details about each file as possible. You may even want to view *thumbnails* — small pictures — that show the contents of image files.

To change the view type, select View and then choose one of the following options:

- The *Large Icons* option displays each file or folder in alphabetically arranged horizontal rows using the same size icons that appear on the Windows Me desktop. All folder icons appear before any file icons.

■ The *Small Icons* option displays the icons in a similar manner, but using much smaller icons that require far less space. Note, however, that in Small Icon view, the entire filename is shown rather than the abbreviated filename shown in Large Icon view, so you may not see any more icons than in Large Icon view.

■ The *List* option displays the icons in a similar manner as the Small Icon view, except that the icons are arranged in vertical columns rather than horizontal rows.

■ The *Details* option displays the icons in a vertical column along with additional columns that provide details, such as the size, type, and date of the files. In Details view, you can choose the display sort order by clicking one of the column headings. You can reverse the order by clicking the same column heading a second time.

■ The *Thumbnails* option displays a small picture of the contents of any image files in the folder. This view enables you to see what is in an image file without first opening the file.

Customizing the display

You can control the Windows Explorer display in many other ways, too. Figure 6-3 shows the View menu that you can use to access these options. You may want to know about these more useful options:

■ Choose View⇨Toolbars⇨Customize to control the display of the labels on the toolbar. Removing the labels shrinks the toolbar. You can always view the name of a toolbar button by holding the mouse pointer over the button for a short time.

Figure 6-3: Customize the Windows Explorer display by using the View menu options.

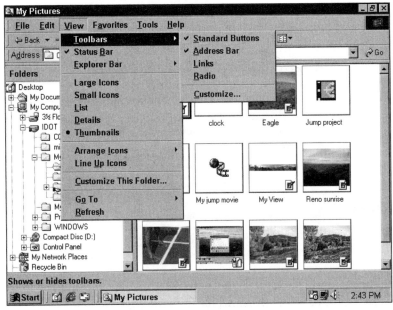

■ Choose View➪Toolbars➪Address Bar to toggle the display of the Address Bar. Removing the Address Bar gives you a bit more room for viewing the files and folders.

■ Choose View➪Arrange Icons to select a different sort order for the current folder.

■ Move the mouse pointer over the vertical divider between the Windows Explorer panes. When the pointer changes to a double-headed arrow, hold down the left mouse button and drag the divider left or right to resize the panes.

■ In Details view, drag the column dividers to resize the columns. Double-click the divider at the right edge of a column to automatically resize the column to show the longest entry.

■ To create the maximum space for the contents pane, click the Close button at the top of the Folders Explorer Bar. You can click the Folders button to redisplay the Folders Explorer Bar when necessary.

Adding and arranging folders

Storing files on your PC is an awful lot like using a filing cabinet to store paperwork. In both cases, you typically use different folders to organize your work.

You can create new folders anywhere on your PC's disk drives, but you need to be aware of one limitation on creating new folders: The *root* folder — the unnamed folder at the lowest level of a disk drive (C:\, for example) — has a limited capacity. You're probably safe if you keep the number of root folder entries under about 100.

One good method of organizing your document files is to use the My Documents folder as the basis for your new folders. There, you can create as many new folders as necessary to organize your document files for different projects. Creating a new folder in Windows Me is quite easy. Follow these steps:

1. Open Windows Explorer.

2. In the Folders Explorer Bar, select the folder that you want as the *parent* of the new folder. This is the folder that will contain your new folder.

3. Choose File⇨New⇨Folder. This creates a folder named New Folder. The name of the new folder is highlighted in the Windows Explorer contents pane.

4. Type a new name for the folder and press Enter.

If you want to move a folder, you can do so the same way that you move individual files. Dragging and dropping folders is generally the easiest way to move them, but you can also select a folder, click the Cut button, select the new parent folder, and click the Paste button.

Moving a folder also moves everything in the folder. If what you really want to do is move the folder's contents but not the folder itself, first select the folder in the Folders Explorer Bar. Then press Ctrl+A to select everything in the folder. Now you can use either the drag-and-drop or the cut-and-paste method to move the selected items, leaving the folder in place.

It is safe to move your document files where you want, but if you move other types of files, you may create problems, such as preventing some programs from running properly. If you need to move a program file, uninstalling the program and then later reinstalling it in the new location is generally the safest way to go. For more info on adding new programs, see Chapter 8.

Using Disks

Nearly every PC has three different types of disk drives. In most cases, drive A: holds 3½-inch removable disks known as *floppy disks* or *diskettes*. Most PCs skip drive B:. Drive C: is a *hard disk* and has a capacity several thousand times that of drive A:. Both of these types of drives are used to store program and document files and are typically available for saving files.

The third common type of drive is the CD-ROM drive, and this is often designated as drive D: (but it can be any letter higher than C). CD-ROMs look very much like audio CDs (and, in fact, CD-ROM drives can usually play audio CDs). In most PCs, the CD-ROM drive is a *read-only* drive — you can read information from the drive but can't save anything to it. Variations on the CD-ROM drive, including CD-R and CD-RW drives, can record data on special discs. Some newer PCs include DVD drives, which use a special high capacity disc.

In addition to these common types of disk drives, some PCs use other types of disk drives, such as Zip drives. Essentially, these other types of drives are simply much higher capacity replacements for floppy disks. You can use these alternative disks only if your system is equipped with the correct type of drive.

Preparing disks for use

Disks must be *formatted* before they can be used. This simply means that electronic markers are placed on the disk so that your system knows where to write the data. Most disks are already formatted and ready to use when you get them.

Warning

Before you format a disk you should be aware that formatting erases everything that is currently on the disk. Don't format a disk unless you're certain that you won't need anything that is on the disk.

Follow these steps to format a disk:

1. Place the disk that you want to format in drive A:.

2. Open Windows Explorer.

3. In the Folders Explorer Bar, right-click the icon for 3½ Floppy (A:). You may need to scroll up a bit to see this icon.

4. Choose Format from the pop-up menu, as shown in Figure 6-4.

5. Select the type of format you want to use:

Quick (erase) simply removes any existing files by marking the space that they occupy as available. You can't use this option if the disk has never been formatted.

Full performs a complete format. This is the best option to choose if you will be storing critical files on the disk because this also checks for errors on the disk.

Figure 6-4:   Choose Format to prepare a disk for use.

6. Type a name of up to 11 characters in the label box. This disk label may help you identify the disk later.

7. Click the Start button to begin formatting the disk.

8. Wait until the format is complete before you click the Close button.

If the Display Summary When Finished check box is checked, Windows Me shows you the results of the formatting process. Disks are cheap — discard any disks that show errors during a format.

Increasing disk performance

Your disk drives are usually some of the slowest parts of your PC. Any performance improvements that you can make may have a large effect on the overall performance of your entire computer system. This list of improvements can include removing files that are simply wasting space and making certain that your files are stored in a manner that allows them to be accessed as quickly as possible.

Windows Me provides some tools specifically to help get the best performance from your disk drives. Access the Windows Me disk tools by following these directions:

1. Open Windows Explorer.

2. In the Folders Explorer Bar, right-click the drive icon for the drive that you want to improve (typically drive C:).

3. Choose Properties from the pop-up menu to display the Properties dialog box for the selected disk.

4. On the General tab, click the Disk Cleanup button.

5. Make certain that all the check boxes are checked and then click OK.

6. Click Yes to remove the extra files (such as the files in the Recycle Bin or temporary Internet files).

7. When you return to the Properties dialog box, click the Tools tab.

8. Click the Check Now button to start the ScanDisk tool. ScanDisk checks to make certain your disk doesn't have any errors that can cause you to lose data.

9. Make certain that the Automatically Fix Errors check box is checked and then click the Start button in the Scan-Disk dialog box.

10. Click the Close button when ScanDisk finishes checking your disk.

11. Click the Defragment Now button to start the disk defragmenter tool. This improves your disk performance by making each file's data *contiguous* (located together) on the hard disk. Defragmenting your hard disk goes much faster if no other programs are running at the same time.

12. Click the Close button when the defragmentation is complete.

13. Click the OK button to close the Properties dialog box.

If you don't want to do your disk maintenance manually every time, you can have Windows Me automatically run these tools. Click the Start button and then choose Programs⇨Accessories⇨SystemTools⇨Maintenance Wizard to set up a schedule for running these tasks on a regular basis. Be sure to choose a time when you won't be using your PC, but when your computer will be powered on.

You can do even more to improve your PC's performance by remembering to delete old files that you no longer need and by resisting the urge to continually add new programs that you don't need to your system.

Finding Files

With the Windows Me Search tool, you can find almost anything on your computer. You can perform these types of searches using the Find tool:

■ You can search for a file even if you know only part of the filename.

■ You can find files that were modified within a specific time period.

■ You can locate all files of a specific type.

■ You can look for files that contain specific text.

■ You can search for files of a certain size.

Follow these steps to use the Search tool on your system:

1. Choose Start⇨Search⇨Files or Folders to display the Search Results window.

2. Enter your search criteria in the various text boxes on the Search pane. In some cases, you need to select an item — such as Date — to view the options that are available.

Remember

Remember that the located files must meet each condition you specify. Start out simple and then restrict the search by adding more conditions if your search produces too many results.

3. Click the Search Now button to begin the search. Depending on the number of files on the drives being searched, the search may take several minutes.

4. If you need to further restrict your search while retaining all the current search conditions, add those new conditions to the appropriate text boxes and click Search Now again without clicking the New button. Clicking New clears the search conditions.

After you locate the file you want, you can work with the file directly in the Search Results window. If you want to open a file, double-click its name in the file list. You can also right-click the files in the list to display the pop-up context menu so that you can rename, delete, cut, or copy them. Depending on the file type, you may have additional options available.

CHAPTER 7

SAVING AND OPENING YOUR WORK

IN THIS CHAPTER

- Saving your files
- Starting your documents
- Recycling your files

You probably spend lots of time working with the documents that you create on your PC. These many hours of effort represent an important investment on your part and make protecting your documents a high priority. In this chapter, you learn how to make certain that your documents are safe and accessible.

Saving Your Files

One of the most confusing topics for new computer users is the difference between *offline* storage — such as disk drives — and memory. Memory is the computer's workspace — the place where programs and data must be moved so that the computer can work with them. Offline storage holds data that won't disappear when the computer is turned off. When you begin work on a new document, that document is first created in memory. Only after it is saved does the document also exist on a disk. If you don't save it, the document completely disappears as soon as you power down the computer.

Remember

Memory and disk space serve quite different purposes. If you don't remember anything else about the two, at least remember that your documents aren't safe until you've saved them to disk.

Saving to the My Documents folder

Windows Me automatically creates a folder — C:\My Documents — for your applications to save your document files. This folder is intended as the place where most of your documents are stored, so most programs that were designed for Windows Me automatically offer the My Documents folder as the default location for saving your files.

In most applications, you save documents by using the File⇨Save command. When you use this command, Windows Me displays the Save dialog box and generally suggests My Documents as the destination. However, if you last saved your files to a different folder, Windows Me usually offers that last folder as the destination.

Tip

You really should look closely at the destination folder named in the Save dialog box. Otherwise, you may have a difficult time finding your files if they weren't saved where you expected them to be.

You should get in the habit of saving your files often so that you have a recent copy if you lose power, your computer crashes, or some other problem makes you lose the work that is in memory. Gauge the time between saves by the amount of work you feel like redoing when problems occur. You may also want to activate any automatic save features in your applications, but generally you experience less hassle if you simply click the Save button every so often.

Saving to the My Pictures folder

In addition to the My Documents folder, Windows Me also creates a folder called My Pictures. If you work with image files, you probably want to save images in the My Pictures folder, which is a subfolder under the My Documents folder.

The My Pictures folder offers a real advantage compared to any other folder as your image file storage location. My Pictures includes a simple image viewer program that enables you to view, zoom, rotate, or print the contents of an image file. Figure 7-1 shows how this viewer enables you to see much more detail than you can easily see in the thumbnail view of a file.

Figure 7-1:   The My Pictures folder includes a handy image viewer.

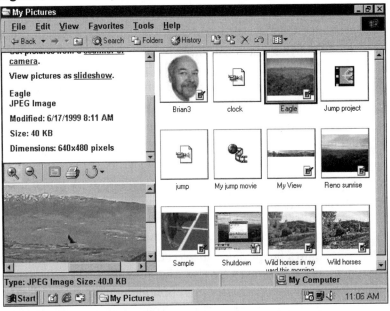

Saving another copy

You might want to save an extra copy of one of your documents for many reasons. You might want to create a new document using much of the same structure and content as an existing document, so your existing document provides a good starting point. You might need to save a copy of a file in a different *file format* for use in a different program. You might even want to turn an existing document into one that can be viewed on a Web page — many modern application programs include this as one of the file saving options.

Nearly all application programs include a Save As command on the File menu. This command is your key to being able to save a file using a different name or a different format.

If you want to share some information from a document with someone who does not have an application that can read your document files, save the document as a plain text file. You lose all the document formatting, but the content remains intact.

Copying files to removable disks

Copying document files onto removable disks — such as floppy disks — is a good way to protect your files from problems that may damage or destroy files on your hard disk. Removable disks can also be a reasonable means of sharing files with other people, especially if you don't have a network.

You can copy files to a floppy disk (or other type of removable disk) in several ways. The method you choose may end up being a compromise between the easiest and the best methods.

The most straightforward method of saving document files onto a floppy disk is to select drive A: as the destination after you choose File⇨Save As. Unfortunately, this tends to cause most programs to set the default file location to drive A:. This means that any new files that you save are also saved onto the floppy disk, and if you attempt to open an existing file, the program insists on looking for that file on drive A: as well. And the same problem may still exist the next time you open the program, too.

A better way to save document files onto a floppy disk is to first save the file as usual in the My Documents folder. When you close the document, double-click the My Documents folder on your desktop. Right-click the document file that you want to copy to a floppy disk, and choose Send To⇨ 3½ Floppy (A). Because this method doesn't change any of the application's default settings, you don't have to hassle with changing anything back to what you really want.

Moving the My Documents folder

If necessary, you can move the My Documents folder — which you might want to do if you need to watch your disk space or if you can use a network drive for your document storage. To make certain that your applications find the new location, though, you must follow the correct procedure:

1. Right-click the My Documents icon on your desktop.

2. Choose Properties from the pop-up context menu.

3. Click the Move button.

4. Select the new location.

5. Click OK to confirm your change.

6. Click OK to close the dialog box.

Be sure to verify the location the next time you save files to make certain that the programs use the correct folder.

Starting Your Documents

Windows Me gives you several different popular methods for opening document files. The following sections show you several of these.

Starting recent files

Windows Me keeps a list of the last 15 documents you've used. To reopen one of these files, click the Start button and then choose Documents. Click the document you want from the list. Windows Me opens the document using the correct application program.

If the document you want is not on the list, click My Documents or My Pictures at the top of the list to see the entire listing of your documents.

Emptying the Recent Documents list

The list of your recently used documents on the Start menu is convenient, but sometimes it might be a little too convenient. Anyone who opens the list can easily see what documents you've been using.

Your list of recently used documents is easily visible to other people on your network, and you won't have any warning that anyone is snooping. This is another good reason that you may want to be concerned about what appears on your recent documents list — especially if you've been working on your resume!

Items on the recent documents list are *shortcuts* to the actual documents. Shortcuts are simply links to another file — they are not the actual file itself. Deleting the shortcut has no effect on the document itself, and deleting or moving the document file has no effect on the shortcut. If you accidentally delete a document file, the shortcut remains on the recent documents list — which may make you think that your document is still safe.

You can clear individual items from the recent documents list, or you can go all the way and take everything off the list. To clear items one at a time, follow these steps:

1. Click the Start button.

2. Choose Documents to open the most recently used documents list.

3. Right-click the item that you want to remove and choose Delete. Hold down the Shift key if you don't want the shortcut moved to the Recycle Bin.

To quickly clear the entire list, follow these steps:

1. Right-click the Windows Me taskbar.

2. Choose Properties to display the Taskbar and Start Menu Properties dialog box.

3. Click the Advanced tab to bring the tab to the front.

4. Click the Clear button to remove your entire list of document shortcuts. This step doesn't send the shortcuts to the Recycle Bin, so be certain that you want to clear the list completely before you click the button.

5. Click the OK button to close the dialog box.

Most Windows Me programs also keep a list of recent documents at the bottom of their File menu, so clearing out the recent documents list may not remove all traces of the files that you've been using.

Starting from the My Documents folder

Because only the 15 most recently used documents can fit on the Start menu list, you will likely find that many of the documents you need to use are not on that list. You can still open any of them quite quickly by first opening the My Documents (or My Pictures) folder. Use one of these quick methods of opening the My Documents folder:

■ You can double-click the My Documents icon on your desktop.

■ You can open Windows Explorer and then open the My Documents folder that appears at the top of the folder list.

■ You can also open the folder by selecting My Documents (or My Pictures) from the top of the recently used documents list on the Start menu.

After you open the My Documents folder, you can simply double-click (or single-click depending on how your system is configured) the document file you want to open. Because Windows Me remembers the correct program to use, you don't have to worry about the document type.

Starting files by clicking

You can also open a document file from within the application program that you used to create the document. Most applications include several options for opening document files:

- Nearly all programs have a File⇨Open command that displays an Open dialog box. Use this dialog box to select the files that you want to open and then click the Open button.

- Many programs include an Open icon on their Standard toolbar, which also displays the Open dialog box.

- You may also see a list of recently used files at the bottom of a program's File menu. Click the file you want to open without going through the Open dialog box.

Starting files by dragging

You can open most documents by dragging and dropping them. This method is especially useful if you want to open the document in a different application than the one Windows Me would normally use for that type of document. For example, you might need to use a special graphics program to work with an image file that you normally open in a different program.

You can use several drag-and-drop techniques to open document files in specific programs:

■ Point to the file that you want to open, hold down the left mouse button, drag the file onto the program you want to use to open the file, and release the mouse button to drop the file.

■ If the target program is open, you drop the file onto the program's window.

■ If you can't see the window, move the mouse pointer over the program's Taskbar button, wait for the program window to open, and then drop the file on the window.

Don't drop documents on the Taskbar button — the file won't open and you'll see an error message.

■ If the target program is not open, you can drop the document file onto the program's icon.

Recycling Files

Anyone can make a mistake, and accidentally deleting an important file is one of those all too common mistakes that everyone makes eventually. To protect you from this type of error, Windows Me provides the Recycle Bin to give you a second chance. The Recycle Bin temporarily stores files you delete so that you can recover them if necessary.

Some files are deleted immediately rather than going to the Recycle Bin:

■ Files that you delete from the MS-DOS Prompt command line are not sent to the Recycle Bin.

■ Files that you delete while holding down the Shift key are not sent to the Recycle Bin.

■ If the Do Not Move Files to the Recycle Bin check box in the Recycle Bin Properties dialog box is selected, no files are sent to the Recycle Bin.

Recovering files from the Recycle Bin

To recover a file you accidentally deleted, open the Recycle Bin as soon as possible and restore the file. You don't want to wait any longer than necessary because the oldest files in the Recycle Bin can be erased to make room for newer ones.

To restore files that you have accidentally deleted, follow these steps:

1. Open the Recycle Bin by double-clicking (or single-clicking as appropriate) the Recycle Bin icon on your desktop.

2. Right-click the item that you want to restore.

3. Choose Restore from the pop-up context menu as shown in Figure 7-2.

4. Click the Close button to close the Recycle Bin.

Figure 7-2: Select Restore to recover an accidentally deleted file.

Restored files are always restored to their original location; so if you have created a new file with the same name in that location, rename the new file before you restore the deleted one.

Emptying the Recycle Bin

The Recycle Bin stores deleted files only as long as it has enough room for newer deletions. If you simply ignore your Recycle Bin, you might not be able to find really important files because they have been replaced by later arrivals. Emptying the Recycle Bin can solve this problem by making additional space.

Use these ways to empty the Recycle Bin:

■ If you want to completely remove all files from the Recycle Bin, open the Recycle Bin and choose File⇨Empty Recycle Bin or click the Empty Recycle Bin button. You can also right-click the Recycle Bin icon on your desktop and choose Empty Recycle Bin from the pop-up context menu.

■ If you want to selectively remove files from the Recycle Bin, open the Recycle Bin and select the files that you want to remove. Then right-click the selected files and choose Delete from the pop-up context menu.

CHAPTER 8

ADDING MORE OF THOSE FUN PROGRAMS

Your PC is a very adaptable machine. All it needs is the right software, and it can play many different roles.

In this chapter, you learn how to install and remove programs, how to make certain that the pieces of Windows Me you need are installed, and how to keep your PC up-to-date with all the latest upgrades from Microsoft.

Installing More Programs

Adding a new program to your PC is usually the best way to gain new features and capabilities. In most cases, you don't need a new PC when you want to do more with your computer — you only need some new software.

Creating a restore point

Installing new programs may give you some new features, but it may also create some new problems. One of the best ways to insure that adding a new program won't result in problems that you can't resolve is to create a *restore point* that you can return to if the new program causes problems.

To create a restore point, follow these steps:

1. Click the Start button, and choose Programs⇨Accessories⇨System Tools⇨System Restore.

2. Click the Create a Restore Point Which I Can Restore to Later option.

3. Type a name for the restore point and click OK.

4. When the message tells you the restore point has been created, click the Done button.

Remember

If you have problems after installing a program, you can return your system to its previous state by selecting the restore point you created. This will remove the program you installed, but not any documents that you created. Click the Start button and choose Programs⇨Accessories⇨System Tools⇨System Restore to open System Restore so that you can select a restore point.

Adding programs

Installing a new program in Windows Me is easy; just follow these steps:

1. Insert the new program's installation CD-ROM into your CD-ROM drive. If the installation program starts automatically, skip to Step 7.

2. If the installation program doesn't run automatically, click the Start button and choose Settings⇨Control Panel.

3. When the Control Panel opens, double-click the Add/Remove Programs icon.

4. In the Add/Remove Programs Properties dialog box that appears, click the Install button on the Install/Uninstall tab.

5. Click the Next button to have Windows Me search for the install program.

6. If the correct program is shown, click the Finish button. If the installation instructions indicate that you should enter a different command than the one shown, do so before you click Finish.

7. Follow the on-screen prompts to complete the installation.

In most cases, you will have a number of choices to make during the installation. Unless you have a reason to do otherwise, choosing the default settings is generally the easiest way to install a program.

If the installation prompts you to register online, use this option so that you will be notified of any program updates.

If some of your existing programs start having problems after you've installed a new program, it's almost always the fault of the new program. Try reinstalling the old programs to see if the problems go away. If that doesn't help, it's time to use your restore point to back out the changes that were made installing the new program.

Removing Programs

Old programs can pile up like a bunch of dirty socks — eventually, they're just eating up space and serving no useful purpose. Removing old programs frees up disk space so that you can add even more new programs or save even more document files.

An old program may be the only one that can open some of your document files. You may want to convert any old documents to a new format before you remove the old program so that you don't lose access to important files.

Most programs can be uninstalled this way:

1. Choose Start⇨Settings⇨Control Panel.

2. Double-click the Add/Remove Programs icon.

3. Select the program you want to uninstall from the list in the bottom section of the Install/Uninstall tab of the Add/Remove Programs Properties dialog box.

4. Click the Add/Remove button.

5. Follow the on-screen directions.

Adding More Windows Features

Lots of different pieces make up Windows Me, and it's pretty likely that some of the interesting components haven't been installed on your system. It's just as likely that some of the items that are installed don't interest you at all. You can pick and choose the Windows Me components you want by using the Add/Remove Programs Properties dialog box.

To control which Windows Me components are installed, click the Start button, choose Settings⇨Control Panel, double-click Add/Remove Programs, and click the Windows Setup tab. Figure 8-1 shows the Windows Setup tab of the Add/Remove Programs Properties dialog box, where you will find the optional components that you can choose to install or remove.

You see a number of different categories of optional components. Each category includes a number of individual items that you can view and select by first selecting the category and then clicking the Details button. Add a check mark in front of any item that you want installed, and remove the check mark to uninstall items. After you make all your choices, click the Apply button to add and remove the optional components. You may need to insert your Windows Me CD-ROM. When the installation is complete, close the dialog box and if prompted, restart your system.

Figure 8-1:   Choose the optional Windows Me components you want.

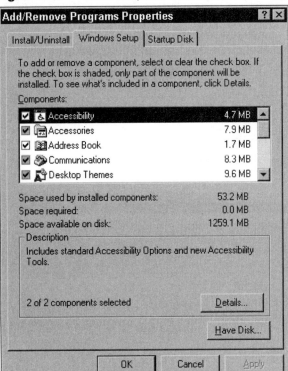

A few of the optional components — such as Briefcase —
cannot be removed after they have been installed, unless you
first create a system restore point.

Using Windows Update and AutoUpdate

Windows Me is a complex collection of software, and this
means that updates will be necessary from time to time. Some
of these updates correct problems that have been discovered,
some protect against new security threats that have emerged,
and some simply add new features to make your PC even
more capable.

Keeping your computer up-to-date could be a complex task if it weren't for a couple of features that are part of Windows Me. The first is Windows Update — which is actually a Microsoft Web site where Windows Me updates are available for download. To use Windows Update, you click the Start button and then choose Windows Update from the top of the Start menu. This starts Internet Explorer and takes you to the Windows Update Web site. Click the Product Updates link and wait while the site determines whether it has any updates available for your system.

If updates are available, they will be divided into several different categories. Any updates marked as critical updates are very important, and you should select them. Other updates are generally listed in decreasing importance, and you can select the ones you want. When you have selected the updates you want to download and install, click the Download button.

Most updates install automatically after they have been downloaded. Be sure to click the "read first" links to make certain that you have any information you need before you download the selected updates.

The one problem with Windows Update is that you have to remember to visit the Windows Update Web site. Windows Me provides a better way to make certain that you know of any critical updates — AutoUpdate. When you activate this feature, Windows Me automatically checks for critical updates whenever you are online. To activate this feature, follow these steps:

1. Click the Start button and choose Settings⇨Control Panel.

2. Double-click the Automatic Updates icon.

3. Select the automatic update option that you prefer.

4. Click OK to activate your choice.

You cannot use the Windows Me update features unless you have registered your copy of Windows Me. Registering Windows Me is usually automatic when you install Windows Me or when you run it for the first time.

CHAPTER 9

GET THEM WHILE THEY'RE FREE — WINDOWS ACCESSORIES

IN THIS CHAPTER

- Using the general purpose accessories
- Using the system tools
- Using the communications accessories

The Windows Me accessory programs cover a broad range of capabilities. You will likely find that some of the accessories are very useful, while others don't interest you at all. This chapter provides you with a quick look at some of the more important accessories without attempting to cover every obscure utility that you would probably never use.

If you see an interesting item in this chapter but cannot find it on your PC, you may want to refer to Chapter 8 for information on installing more of Windows Me. Some of the Windows Me accessories simply aren't installed by default, so you may need to step in and take a minute to install some of them yourself.

Sampling Windows Programs

Windows Me has several accessories that you may use fairly often. These are tools you'll find by clicking the Start button and choosing Programs⇨Accessories.

Writing with Notepad

Notepad is a *text editor* — a program that you use to edit or create plain text files. Windows Me uses a number of files that must be plain text without any formatting, and Notepad is generally a good choice for working with these files because Notepad won't add any special characters that can cause problems in these files.

Some of the files you might edit with Notepad include the following:

- *Configuration files* — special files that hold settings that enable your hardware and software to function correctly on your system

- *Log files* — files that contain the results of certain operations, such as program installations or the errors encountered while attempting to perform tasks

Notepad cannot open files that are very large. But if you attempt to open a text file that is too large for Notepad, Windows Me asks whether you would like to open the file in WordPad. If you do, remember to save any changes in the same plain-text format so that the file is not damaged.

Writing with WordPad

WordPad also allows you to edit files, but it has far more features and capabilities than Notepad does. WordPad is essentially a slimmed down version of Microsoft Word. With WordPad, you can open and save Word documents, apply formatting, and generally produce a fairly nice-looking document without the hassle of dealing with a full-blown word processor.

WordPad, of course, lacks some of the features common to complete word processing programs. You won't, for example, find a spell checker, mail merge capabilities, or macro programming. But in some ways, this lack of features can be an advantage because WordPad can be used to open Word documents without worrying about any macro viruses that might be contained in the file.

If you don't have Microsoft Word installed on your system, you can use WordPad to open Word documents that someone sends you. This enables you to view and print the document with the original formatting intact.

Drawing pictures

Most of the images you see on your computer screen are *bitmap images* — graphic images that use small individual blocks, or *pixels*, to form a picture. If you want to create or modify bitmap images, you can use Paint, an editor that can work with several different image formats, including both BMP and JPEG files.

When you open Paint, you see a series of tools in a tool palette along the left edge of the Paint window. Along the bottom of the window, you see a set of color selection boxes. You use these tools and color selection palettes to create or modify images in much the same way you might use cans of spray paint or colored pens to paint a picture.

With Paint you can modify any of the image files that can be used as Windows Me desktop wallpaper. You can, for example, crop out part of the image if you want to use only part of it.

Scanning images

Imaging is a program that you can use to scan images with your scanner or import images from your digital camera. You can also work with faxes that you want to send or with faxes that you have received. Using the annotation tools in Imaging, you can add comments or otherwise mark up an image. For example, you can draw attention to an important point in a fax when you send a response.

Unlike Paint, Imaging allows you to have several images open at the same time — such as a multiple-page fax. When you're working with multiple page documents in Imaging, you may want to click the Page and Thumbnails View button to display each page of the document using a small thumbnail view and the currently selected page in a normal-sized view. To switch to a different page, you can simply click the thumbnail of the page you want to view.

Tip

Imaging can open many more types of files than is possible in Paint. If you have an image file in a format that Windows Me cannot use as desktop wallpaper, open the image in Imaging and then save it in BMP format. You will then be able to use the image as wallpaper.

Calculating

If you need to do some quick calculations, you don't have to look any further than the Windows Me Calculator program. This accessory has both standard and scientific modes, as well as memory functions.

Tip

You can copy and paste values between the Calculator and other Windows Me applications. Copying and pasting the result of a calculation reduces the possibility of making an error when entering it into a document.

To use the Calculator, you can enter numbers by using the number keys on your keyboard or by clicking the buttons on the Calculator itself. You need to click the buttons to use most of the functions. You use the View menu to switch between the standard and scientific modes.

Figure 9-1 shows the Calculator in scientific mode. In this figure, the pi button was clicked to demonstrate the precision that is available.

Figure 9-1:   The Windows Me Calculator is a quick and convenient tool
for performing precise calculations.

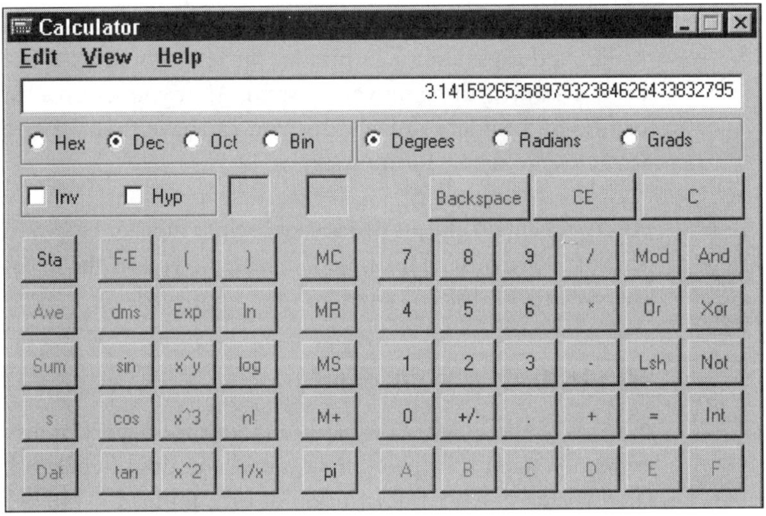

Housekeeping

The next group of Windows Me accessories are tools that you
find on the Programs⇨Accessories⇨System Tools menu.
These are tools that you can use to keep your PC running
efficiently and to avoid problems that might cause you to lose
important data.

Archiving your files

Backing up your important files can help protect you from
problems with your computer hardware and from user errors
as well. Windows Me includes a program called Backup that
you can use to easily make the copies you need. If your PC
has a tape backup drive, Backup uses the tape drive for backups. Most tapes have fairly high capacity, so you can typically
start a backup and walk away. You can also back up to floppy
disks, if that is your only option.

When you use Backup, you can choose specific files and folders that you want to save, which is important because a partial backup that saves your data files is really all that you need. And a partial backup takes far less time than a full backup of everything on your system. After you set up a list of files and folders to back up, you can save that list as a *backup set* to use in future backups.

Always maintain at least two sets of backup disks or tapes and alternate their use. This practice protects you in the event that one set of disks or tapes becomes damaged.

Maintaining your disks

Several Windows Me accessories fall into the category of disk tools. These tools help you maintain the health of your disk drives. Here is a brief description of each tool:

- *Disk Cleanup* is a tool that removes unneeded files from your hard disk to free up the space that they're wasting.

- *Disk Defragmenter* is a tool that makes your hard disk more efficient by rearranging your files. Defragmenting makes reading your files more efficient and improves the performance of your system.

- *ScanDisk* is a tool that looks for and corrects trouble on your disk drives.

Although you can run the disk tools manually, it is usually preferable to use the Maintenance Wizard discussed in the next section to schedule these tools to run automatically when you aren't using your PC.

Scheduling tasks

Certain tasks — such as disk maintenance — are extremely important if you want your PC to keep running at its best.

Windows Me can help by running those tasks automatically on a regular schedule.

Windows Me includes two tools that make scheduling routine maintenance much easier. The *Task Scheduler* (which appears as Scheduled Tasks on the Start menu) automatically runs programs at specified times. The *Maintenance Wizard* helps you create routine maintenance tasks within the Task Scheduler. For example, you might schedule the Disk Defragmenter to run every couple of days to make certain your system is running at peak efficiency.

You can view the current task schedule by double-clicking the Task Scheduler icon in the system tray. When the Task Scheduler is open, you can also create new tasks or modify the schedule for existing ones.

The Maintenance Wizard schedules tasks that can make your PC run more efficiently. You can choose to use express mode or custom mode to schedule these tasks. Express mode is somewhat easier, of course, but it doesn't give you as much control or information as custom mode does.

Your PC must be powered on at the time when scheduled tasks are set to run — otherwise, the Task Scheduler won't be able to run the tasks.

Finding system information

The System Information tool provides a wealth of detail about your PC. It shows you information about your hardware, the software that is running, and any drivers that may be loaded. This tool is actually the gateway to several important tools. As Figure 9-2 shows, the Tools menu provides access to a number of programs that you can use to diagnose and correct problems that you may encounter.

Figure 9-2: The System Information Tools menu provides several powerful options for maintaining your PC.

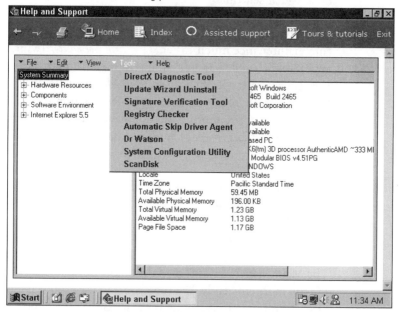

The System Information display provides lots of information about your computer. If you are having problems with your system, you can copy the information about items such as *IRQs, DMA channels,* and *I/O addresses* into an e-mail message to a technical support person. Alternatively, you can click the printer icon to print out the currently displayed System Information branch — each branch provides information on specific areas of your computer.

Many of the options on the Tools menu provide access to programs that can potentially damage your system. If you don't know what you are doing, it is safest to leave these options alone unless someone who is a system expert is helping you.

Inserting special characters

If you need to use foreign characters or other special symbols in your documents, the Character Map can make the process far simpler. This tool (also accessed from the System Tools menu) enables you to easily insert special characters into your documents.

You can copy characters to the Character Map scratchpad by double-clicking the character or by clicking the Select button. If you want to enter a symbol rather than a normal character, select a symbol font, such as Symbol or Wingdings. When you have copied all the characters you need, click the Copy button so that you can close Character Map and copy the characters into your document.

After you click a character, use the arrow keys to move the magnifier through the character set.

Don't change the font of the characters that you've copied into your document. Changing the font may result in a different character being displayed.

If you need to insert several special characters into the same document, it may be easier to insert them all at once and then move them around, rather than switching back and forth between your document and the Character Map several times.

Communicating

Windows Me has several communications tools on the Start⇨Programs⇨Accessories⇨Communications section of the Start menu.

Connecting through Dial-up Networking

Dial-up Networking is essential for connecting to the Internet, but that isn't its only purpose. As the name implies, you use Dial-up Networking to establish a remote connection to a network — often through a modem. When you set up an account with an Internet service provider, Windows Me creates a Dial-up Networking connection that contains all the parameters necessary to successfully establish that connection.

To open the Dial-up Networking folder, click the Start button and choose Settings⇨Dial-up Networking. You can use the New Connection icon to create a new dial-up connection, or you can open an existing connection by double-clicking the appropriate connection icon. If you want to modify the properties for a connection, right-click the connection icon and choose Properties from the pop-up context menu.

Setting up your home network

If you have two or more PCs, you probably have the need to share files between those systems on occasion. You can select the Home Networking Wizard to set up the necessary network *protocols* and services to quickly get your network up and running.

Your PCs need the proper hardware to be networked. You can find inexpensive kits that include the adapters, cables, and hub you need for a simple network. These kits are available at most office supply and computer stores.

Sharing an Internet connection

If you have a home network, you don't need a separate Internet connection for each PC. You can save money by sharing a single Internet connection because only one PC needs to be connected to the Internet, and you can typically share a single account.

To share an Internet connection, your PCs must be networked. If they are, you use Internet Connection Sharing to set up one PC as the *gateway* that provides Internet access to the rest of the PCs on the network. When you install Internet Connection Sharing on your Windows Me system, a floppy disk is created to use in setting up the remaining PCs.

Only one PC on your network can have Internet Connection Sharing installed. The remaining PCs then access the Internet through your network.

CHAPTER 10

PUTTING IT ALL ON PAPER

IN THIS CHAPTER

- Printing
- Installing printer drivers

Printing documents is one of those tasks that is common to most Windows Me applications. The same procedures — with only minor variations — apply no matter what type of document you are printing.

Printing

The easy, no-nonsense way to print in most Windows programs is to use the Print button — the one with the picture of a printer — on the toolbar. Clicking this button usually results in printing one copy of the current document to the default printer, using the default printer settings.

If you want more control over the way that a document prints — which printer it prints to, the number of copies, and so on — choose File⇨Print to bring up the Print dialog box (see Figure 10-1).

Remember

You can use a printer only if the necessary *printer drivers* are installed. If the printer that you want to use is not shown in the Name list box on the Print dialog box, the driver is probably not installed. Driver installation is covered later in this chapter.

Figure 10-1: Use the Print dialog box to control how your documents print.

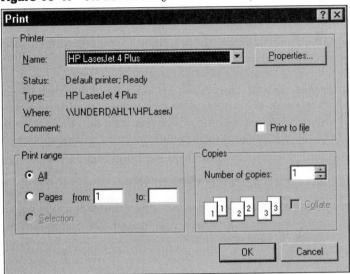

To save paper and ink, use the Print Preview option to make sure that your document will print the way you want it to. Just click the Print Preview button on the toolbar — the one with the paper and magnifying glass — or choose File⇨ Print Preview.

The Print dialog box

You can use the options on the Print dialog box to control just how your document is printed. Consider these important options:

■ To print to a printer other than the default, click the down arrow next to the Name box and select another printer.

■ To change the number of copies you want to print, use the arrows next to Number of Copies. You can also highlight the number in the Number of Copies box and type in the number of copies you want.

- To change which pages you want to print, choose from the options in the Page Range area.

- If you're printing more that one copy of a multi-page document, click the Collate check box to save yourself lots of sorting and collating time.

Click OK in the Print dialog box to print your document with your new settings. Click Cancel if you don't want to print the document right now.

The Page Setup dialog box

Most applications also allow you to control a number of options that relate to paper size, margins, layout, and so on. Typically, you use File⇨Page Setup to open the Page Setup dialog box, but you may have to search a little in some programs to find the correct command.

These common page setup options may vary, depending on your printer and the program from which you're printing:

- To print on different sized paper, click the down arrow next to the Size box and choose a new paper size. Make sure that the size you choose matches the paper that you loaded into your printer.

- To switch between multiple paper sources, select which one to use from the Source drop-down list. This option is especially handy if you have a printer with plain paper in one tray and letterhead paper in another.

- To change the page orientation, choose either landscape or portrait. Portrait orientation is what you're used to — the shorter edge of the paper is at the top and bottom. Landscape turns the paper on its side — the longer edge is on the top and bottom. Use landscape for documents that are too wide to fit on a portrait-oriented page.

- To change how much blank space is between the edge of the paper and the text of the document, type new values in the Top, Bottom, Left, or Right boxes of the Margins area.

Installing Printer Drivers

Windows Me uses printer drivers — software specific to each type of printer — to communicate with your printer. These printer drivers enable Windows Me to use the special features that are available in a printer so that you can print more than simple text on your printer.

To use a printer, you must tell Windows Me to look for it. That's called *installing the printer*. The correct printer drivers are added to your computer during installation. Make sure that you have your Windows CD handy when performing the following steps. If a CD is included with your printer, you need that CD, too.

1. Choose Start⇨Settings⇨Printers. The Printers window appears with an icon for each printer installed on your computer, as shown in Figure 10-2.

Figure 10-2: The printer icons enable you to control or add printers.

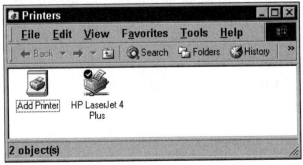

2. Double-click the Add Printer icon to start the Add Printer Wizard.

3. Click Next.

4. Select Local printer to tell Windows that the printer is attached to your computer.

5. Click Next.

6. Select the company that made your printer from the Manufacturers list and then select the correct model of your printer from the Printers list.

7. Click Next.

8. Select the LPT1: option to tell Windows that the printer is connected to your printer port.

9. Click Next.

10. Type a name for your printer, or accept the default name. If you plan to use this printer most often, click Yes to set it as your default printer. If you have more than one printer and this printer won't be the primary printer, click No.

11. Click Next.

12. Click Yes and then click Finish to have Windows print a test page. If Windows can't find the required files on your hard disk, Windows asks you to place either your Windows CD in the CD-ROM drive or the CD that came with your printer. Click OK after you have done so.

13. After Windows prints the test page, click Yes if the page printed successfully.

14. Click the Close button in the upper-right corner of the printer window. Now you're all set to print!

CLIFFSNOTES REVIEW

Use this CliffsNotes Review to practice what you've learned in this book and to build your confidence in doing the job right the first time. After you work through the review questions, the problem-solving exercises, and the fun and useful practice projects, you're well on your way to achieving your goal of using Windows Me confidently.

Q&A

1. How should you exit from an application that's running?

   a. Push the Reset button.

   b. Save your work and then close the program.

   c. Click the lower-left corner of your screen.

   d. Turn the computer off.

2. What happens when you click a menu name?

   a. Nothing; you have to use the keyboard to use menus.

   b. A menu that's open on-screen closes.

   c. A menu appears, showing commands you can click.

   d. Both b and c.

3. How do you start a program?

   a. Use the mouse to highlight its name and then press Enter.

   b. Find the program in your computer's directory of folders and double-click its name.

   c. Type the program's name at the command prompt and press Enter.

   d. All the above.

4. What happens first when your computer starts up?

   a. A built-in program starts the operating system.

   b. Your user interface appears on the screen.

   c. The computer prints out a test document.

   d. The document you're working on appears.

5. How often should you save your work?

   a. Every 10 to 15 minutes.

   b. Every two or three hours.

   c. Weekly.

   d. Never; computers are completely reliable.

6. Which of these methods can you use to transfer files from the C: drive to a floppy-disk drive labeled B:?

   a. From drive C:, select the files you want and then double-click the first one.

   b. Open a window for each drive, select files in the drive C: window, press and hold down the left mouse button, move the mouse pointer over to the drive B: window, and release.

   c. Open a window for the B: drive, use the mouse to select files in the drive C: window, and then type **copy these files to B:**.

   d. Write down the names of the files you want to copy, close the user interface, reboot the computer, and then type **copy to B:** at the command prompt, followed by the file names.

7. How can you determine whether an application is appropriate to run on your PC?

   a. Read about it in a computer magazine.

   b. Check the system requirements on the software box.

   c. Know which peripherals are installed in your system.

   d. All the above.

8. What is the best approach to buying a PC?

   a. See it advertised on TV at a great price and go buy it.

   b. Buy as many features and devices as you can afford.

   c. Always buy state-of-the-art equipment and upgrade every 6 months.

   d. Decide what you want to use a PC for, find the software that will do it, and look for a PC that runs the software well.

Answers: (1) b. (2) d. (3) d. (4) a. (5) a. (6) b. (7) d. (8) d.

Scenarios

1. You finished a letter to a friend and saved it, but when you open your word processor, you can't find it. How can you find your letter? _____

_____

_____

2. You bring home a new laser printer for your computer and connect it to your system, but when you try to print a document, nothing happens. What can you do to fix the problem?

_____

_____

Answers: (1) Use your computer's file-management utility program (such as Windows Explorer or File Manager) to show you the directory tree; use the utility's Search (or similar) command to hunt for the filename of your letter; when you find the letter, save it to a specific folder (most Windows users can use the My Documents folder). (2) Make sure the correct device driver for your printer is installed; the printer should include a disk that has the driver program and instructions that tell you how to install it.

Visual Test

Which of the ports at the back of your computer connect to the printer, the monitor, the mouse, and the Internet? Sketch them, and check your cables to make sure that they are correct for each port.

Consider This

What tasks are you doing now that would go faster and easier on a computer? Which tasks are easier if you use pen and paper? What kind of work is best suited to a computer?

Practice Project

Use your word processor to create your résumé and give it a professional look:

1. Start your word processor.

2. Start a new document in your word processor.

3. Place a clean copy of your old résumé on a copy stand next to your screen.

4. Type the text of your résumé into your on-screen document.

5. Use your word processor's paragraph-formatting commands to left-align your résumé list items and to center-align your section headings.

6. To preserve the work you've done so far, save your document with the title **myresume.doc**.

7. Use your mouse or keyboard to select the entire document, and then use your word processor's character-formatting commands to select a businesslike font for your résumé.

8. Spell-check your résumé, and edit it for grammar and accuracy.

9. Save your résumé twice more — once to a directory on your hard drive (most Windows users can use the My Documents directory), and once to a formatted floppy disk so that you have a backup copy. Then print out and file the updated résumé.

CLIFFSNOTES RESOURCE CENTER

The learning doesn't need to stop here. CliffsNotes Resource Center shows you the best of the best — links to the best information in print and online about Windows Me. Look for these terrific resources at your favorite bookstore or local library and on the Internet. When you're online, make your first stop www.cliffsnotes.com, where you can find even more incredibly useful information about Windows Me.

Books

This CliffsNotes book is one of many great books for PC users from IDG Books Worldwide, Inc. So if you want some great next-step books, check out these other publications:

Windows 98 Bible, by Alan Simpson, is a full-featured reference that includes a CD-ROM full of software tools. IDG Books Worldwide, Inc. $39.99.

PC Upgrade and Repair Simplified, by Ruth Maran, is a guide to maintaining and improving your PC. IDG Books Worldwide, Inc. $24.99.

You can easily find books published by IDG Books Worldwide, Inc., in your favorite bookstores, at the library, on the Internet, and at a store near you. We also have three Web sites that you can use to read about all the books that we publish:

- www.cliffsnotes.com
- www.dummies.com
- www.idgbooks.com

Internet

Check out these Web resources for more information on Windows Me.

Microsoft Windows Update, windowsupdate.microsoft.com, takes you directly to the latest official news from Microsoft about Windows.

Microsoft Download Center, www.microsoft.com/downloads/search.asp, takes you to free downloadable enhancements for Windows Me.

Windows Users Group Network, www.wugnet.com, has a wealth of unofficial, practical information about using a variety of Windows operating systems.

Next time you're on the Internet, don't forget to drop by www.cliffsnotes.com. We created an online Resource Center that you can use today, tomorrow, and beyond.

Magazines and Other Media

PC World, at your local newsstand, shows you the latest news and tips for your PC and how changes in the software industry affect it. Sample its wares at www.pcworld.com.

Windows Magazine covers the world of Windows; hardware, software, buying, testing, comparing. Visits its Web site at www.winmag.com.

Send Us Your Favorite Tips

In your quest for knowledge, have you ever experienced that sublime moment when you figure out a trick that saves time or trouble? Perhaps you realized that you were taking ten steps to accomplish something that could take two. Or you found a little-known workaround that achieved great results. If you've discovered a useful tip that helped you use Windows Me more effectively, and you'd like to share it, the Cliffs staff would love to hear from you. Go to our Web site at www. cliffsnotes.com, and look for the Talk to Us button. If we select your tip, we may publish it as part of *CliffsNotes Daily*, our exciting, free e-mail newsletter. To find out more or to subscribe to a newsletter, go to www.cliffsnotes.com on the Web.

INDEX

I

Imaging, 95
input devices, 6. *See also* mouse
  multiple, 6
installing printer drivers, 107–108
instant messaging, 34–35
interface, 4
  mouse, 4
Internet
  account setup, 22–23
  connecting, 21–22, 24–26
  history of, 20–21
  instant messaging, 34–35
Internet Connection Sharing, 102
Internet Explorer
  address toolbar, 29
  History list, 30
ISPs (Internet Service Providers)
  account information, 23–24
  selecting, 22–23

K

keyboard
  programs, switching between, 18
  setup, 10–11
  shortcuts, 10

M

Maintenance Wizard, 99
menu, Start, 15
monitor, display, improving, 53–54
mouse, 4. *See also* input devices
  changing button functions, 9
  clicking, 6, 8
  moving/copying objects, 8–9
  scrolling screens, 7
  setup, 6
  third button, 7
  wheel, 7
Movie Maker, 43–46
moving
  My Documents folder, 79
  objects with mouse, 8–9
MS-DOS prompt, 17
MSN Messenger, 34–35

multimedia, 36–38, 40–41, 43, 46
  recording, 42–43
music CDs, playing, 39
My Documents folder, moving, 79

N

Notepad, 94

O

operating systems, 3
  compatibility, 11

P

Paint, 95
pictures, saving, 76
pointer (mouse), alternatives, 6
pointing sticks, 6
printer drivers, installing, 107–108
printing, 104
  setup, 105–107
  Web pages, 31–32
programs, 3, 12–13
  accessories, 93–95, 97–103
  closing, 18–19
  documents, 13
  icons, opening with, 15–16
  installing, 86–88
  multiple, running, 18
  operating systems, 3
  removing, 88–89
  restore points, 86
  Run dialog box, opening with, 17
  running, 13–14
  Windows Explorer, opening with, 16

R

recent documents list, clearing, 80–81
recording, 42–43
Recycle Bin, emptying, 84
restore points, 86
roller balls, 6
Run dialog box, 17
running, programs, 13–14

NOTES

NOTES

NOTES